ORGANIZATIONAL PLANNING AND CONTROL SYSTEMS

JAMES C. EMERY

Organizational Planning

Theory an

nd Control Systems

echnology

AN ARKVILLE PRESS BOOK

The Macmillan Company
Collier-Macmillan Limited LONDON

For Posh

First Printing

Library of Congress catalog card number: 69–11106

THE MACMILLAN COMPANY
COLLIER-MACMILLAN CANADA, LTD., Toronto, Ontario

PRINTED IN THE UNITED STATES OF AMERICA

PREFACE

Planning is a universal component of management. And yet, to a considerable extent, it is not well understood by those who practice it. Many managers fancy themselves men of action and view planning as an "unproductive" paperwork activity. In fact, however, it is primarily through planning that a high-level manager exerts influence over his organization.

Although there persists a general lack of appreciation of the planning function, considerable progress has been made in gaining a better understanding of its role (Goetz, 1949; Newman, 1951; Koontz and O'Donnell, 1964). We have also witnessed in recent years great strides in the allied field of organization theory (March and Simon, 1958; Cyert and March, 1963). The progress made in these more traditional areas of management has been accompanied by an explosive expansion of knowledge in the related fields of cybernetics, systems theory, decision theory, and information technology.

Despite this substantial progress, our understanding of organizational planning and control remains far from complete. We are victims of a cultural lag: advances in the traditional and technical fields have not been sufficiently amalgamated to form a unified theory of planning. The lack of such theory accounts, in part, for some of the difficulties that have been encountered in applying information technology in organizations.

I have attempted in this book to achieve a synthesis of the fields related to planning. In doing so I have borrowed shamelessly from both traditional and theoretical literature. Much of what I have written is not especially new, a fact I have tried to indicate by a profusion of references to past work. On the other hand, I would like to think that the resulting synthesis provides a fresh and useful way of viewing organizational planning.

In order to understand the planning process one must understand the concept of systems. Planning exists within an organization, and the organization itself constitutes a system. Accordingly, the first two chapters are devoted to the general topic of the organization as a system—its characteristics, its structure, and the means by which it governs itself.

Formal planning requires information processing. The way planning is carried out therefore depends heavily on the current state of information technology. Chapter 3 covers the role of the information system in an organization. The intent is not to give merely a "state of the art" discussion; rather, it is to provide a systematic view of information systems in order to place planning in the proper context within the information system as a whole.

The zeal of the determined planner must be tempered by economic realities. Planning, like all information processing, yields an output that has both a value and a cost. Chapter 4 gives a conceptual discussion of the economics of information. The theoretical model used for this purpose is designed to illustrate in quantitative terms the issues involved in setting the limits on planning.

This groundwork lays the foundation for the central theme of the book, the planning process. The final chapter provides a construct of planning that is intended to characterize any planning process whether it involves elaborate formal procedures or very informal methods. The intent is to give deeper insight into the fundamental nature of the planning process. The executive, the planner, and the designer of a planning system should approach their tasks with a clear viewpoint about the role of planning. The construct that represents this viewpoint must meet two tests.

First, it must somehow provide a useful set of abstractions that facilitate thinking about the planning process. It should therefore be general enough to encompass a wide variety of planning, and it should be concise enough to become a ready part of the designer's vocabulary of thought. This makes it easier to perceive an overall rationale behind the complex network of planning that takes place within any organization. In the absence of such a point of view, each planning task appears as a special case rather than as part of a unified whole.

Second, the construct should incorporate the best of our available wisdom about planning. It should be capable of explaining or justifying what we consider to be good planning practice. It should also be consistent with current theoretical knowledge.

I have tried to satisfy these criteria in developing a construct of planning. Although the discussion is perhaps somewhat conceptual—I hesitate to use the word "theoretical"—practical ends certainly motivated its development. My real goal is to provide a framework for the implementation of formalized man–machine planning systems. The first step in doing this, I submit, is the formulation of a suitable "world view" about the planning process. Nothing is so practical as good theory.

I owe a huge debt to a host of authors whose works have enriched the fields of organization theory, planning, and information technology. It is impossible to mention them all, but I would like to acknowledge a special personal intellectual debt to the few on whose writing I have depended most heavily: Mr. C. J. Hitch and Professors Billy Goetz, Jacob Marschak, H. A. Simon, and Zenon Zannetos. I am especially grateful to Professors Goetz and Zannetos for their personal help. Both of them provided painstaking care in reviewing the manuscript during its development. Their suggestions and criticisms have contributed substantially to whatever merits the book possesses. Would that I could share any of the book's weaknesses as legitimately as I can share its strengths; its faults, unfortunately, are my responsibility alone.

Various versions of the manuscript were typed by Sandra Litchman, Arlene Stocek, Mary McCutcheon, and Katherine Cooper. For this I thank them all very warmly.

J. C. E.

Philadelphia

STUDIES OF THE MODERN CORPORATION

Columbia University Graduate School of Business

The program for Studies of the Modern Corporation is devoted to the advancement and dissemination of knowledge about the corporation. Its publications are designed to stimulate inquiry, research, criticism, and reflection. They fall into four categories: works by outstanding businessmen, scholars, and professional men from a variety of backgrounds and academic disciplines; prize-winning doctoral dissertations relating to the corporation; edited selections of business literature; and business classics that merit republication. The studies are supported by outside grants from private business, professional, and philanthropic institutions interested in the program's objectives.

Richard Eells
EDITOR

CONTENTS

CHAPTER 1

The Systems Concept 1

Examples of Systems / Characteristics of a System / System Structure

CHAPTER 2

The Organization As a System 20

The Hierarchical Structure of Organizations / Interactions Among Organizational Subunits / Coordination Among Subunits

CHAPTER 3

The Technology of Information Systems 34

The Role of the Information System / Functions Within the Information System / Integrated Information Systems

CHAPTER 4

Economics of Information 66

A Theoretical Model / An Example / Deficiencies in the Theoretical Model / Quantitative Analysis of Information Value / Qualitative Evaluation of Value and Cost

CHAPTER 5

Planning and Control   108

*The Role of Plans   /   Planning Goals   /   The
Hierarchical Nature of Planning   /   The Iterative
Nature of Planning   /   Geometric Interpretation
of Planning   /   The Planning Process at a Given
Level   /   Economics of Planning   /   Man–
Machine Planning   /   Conclusions*

Bibliography   158

Index   165

CHAPTER 1

The Systems Concept

$\mathbf{M}$ANAGING a large organization is fundamentally a matter of coping with complex systems. The organization itself constitutes a system, and it is governed by means of a system of plans. Therefore, in order to gain a real understanding of the planning and control process within an organization, one must first understand the concept of a system.

The dictionary defines a system as "an assemblage of objects united by some form of regular interaction or interdependence." Powers, Clark, and McFarland (1960, pp. 63–65); Hall (1962, pp. 59–68); and Johnson, Kast, and Rosenzweig (1967, p. 4) give similar definitions. Ackoff (1963, p. 121) defines a system as a complex of *interrelated entities* and thus includes conceptual systems as well as concrete ones. There is little point in adding to these definitions, but it does seem worthwhile at least to cite examples of systems and to examine their most important characteristics.

1.1 *Examples of Systems*

The universe abounds with systems: they are ubiquitous. It is perhaps an open philosophical question whether the multitude of systems have an

1

objective reality or merely exist in the mind of the beholder. In any case, man can apparently understand and cope with his complex world only by viewing it in terms of a hierarchy of components (Simon, 1962, p. 477). By organizing his universe in this hierarchical[1] fashion, he need come to terms with only a small portion of it at one time. He can gain some understanding of increasingly larger systems by understanding the aggregate behavior of their major components and the interactions among them.

Systems may be either concrete or abstract. Concrete systems are composed of physical objects. An air defense system, a computer, and a telephone network (Hall, 1962, pp. 23–58) provide examples of man-made concrete systems. Concrete biological systems also exist. For example, the mammalian central nervous system consists of a hierarchy of interacting parts (Bishop, 1960). The physical universe itself may be viewed as a gigantic supersystem composed of a hierarchy of galaxies, solar systems and planets. Speculation about its highest levels falls within the province of the cosmologist (and theologian); the physicist is concerned with the elementary particles that terminate the hierarchy.

Abstract systems arise through man's striving to comprehend the complex. There is good evidence that we habitually factor complex problems into less complex subproblems (Newell, Shaw, and Simon, 1959, pp. 35–41). Through repetition of this process, the subproblems eventually become solvable. Hopefully, the composite solution of the hierarchy of subproblems represents a satisfactory solution of the global problem (Alexander, 1964; Manheim, 1964).

Abstract hierarchies are manifested in many ways. Human knowledge is often organized in these terms. A given branch of knowledge, such as chemistry, exhibits a hierarchical structure of subbranches. At a more detailed level, any author wishing to be understood organizes his ideas in hierarchical form. To further clarify the material, he makes the structure all the more explicit by such means as chapter and section headings and transition sentences. Computer programs have a definite hierarchical structure, and the more explicit this structure, the easier it is to understand, implement, and modify the programs (Simon, 1960, p. 42; Emery, 1962).

All human organizations of any size have a clearly hierarchical struc-

---

[1] Like Simon (1962, p. 468), I use the term *hierarchical* to describe an entity composed of subentities which, in turn, are composed of still lower-level subentities. The process of hierarchical subdivision continues until ultimately some lowest-level elementary subentity is reached. Hierarchy defined in this way does not necessarily imply authority relationships, although higher-level entities often exercise "control" or authority over lower-level subentities. More is said about this in Section 3.1.

ture. The set of plans used to govern an organization also constitutes an exceedingly elaborate hierarchical system. A great deal more will be said about this in later chapters.

Thus we see systems all around us. Whether they *are* systems or whether we only perceive them to be is irrelevant. Man universally thinks in hierarchical terms as a way of whittling down his complex world into more comprehensible form. If systems did not exist we would invent them.

1.2 *Characteristics of a System*

The essential characteristic of a system is that it is composed of interacting parts, each of which has interest in its own right (Ackoff, 1961, p. 28). Without these interactions the study of systems would be relatively uninteresting. It is the interactions that add great richness to the behavior of a system and make the analysis of this behavior an exceedingly complex task.

The parts of a system are themselves composed of subparts. One of the constituent parts of a computer, for example, is the central processing unit, which in turn is composed of various arithmetic circuits and registers. Each of these is made of still finer components. Thus systems universally exhibit a hierarchical structure having parts within parts within parts.

The components of a system are linked through various *interfaces*. These take the form of inputs and outputs. An input or output may be either a physical entity—material or energy—or information.[2] A given system component transforms inputs into outputs, presumably in a way that contributes to the accomplishment of a desired purpose of the system (if, indeed, a purpose motivated the creation of the system). The transformation may, of course, be exceedingly complex, requiring for any real understanding a further breakdown of the component into still finer subcomponents. In many systems, the primary transformation deals with physical inputs and outputs, with information serving only as a means of coordination. On the other hand, a system may deal only with information, as in a management information system (which, of course, is only a subsystem of the organization as a whole).

[2] Information must, of course, be represented in some physical form, such as a printed page or a series of magnetic spots or electrical pulses. However, the information content of a message remains invariant with respect to its physical form. The recognition of this seemingly obvious fact has been a major contribution of information theory (McDonough, 1963, p. 14).

A component is perfectly well defined when one knows the way in which inputs are transformed into outputs. In the presence of interactions among subsystems, however, a knowledge of each component's individual behavior is not sufficient to predict the behavior of the system as a whole (Purcell, 1963, p. 11). A complete description of the system's behavior requires a knowledge of the interrelationships among components as well as the behavior of each component.[3] In the case of a system, the whole is, in a sense, greater than the sum of its parts.

The boundaries of a system are essentially arbitrary (Simon, 1962, p. 468). One can view any branch of a system's hierarchy as a system itself. For example, a computer can be considered an independent system—as it might be by a project engineer responsible for its design. In other cases, the computer would be viewed as only a subsystem in a much larger system— as a component, say, of an air defense system composed of computers, radar equipment, display devices, and communications equipment. The air defense system, in turn, represents only a part of the U.S. Air Force, which is only a part of the Defense Department. This game of building larger systems from smaller ones can go on almost indefinitely. Where one stops this process depends on one's interests and point of view.

The lowest-level terminal points in a system's hierarchy are also essentially arbitrary. One can continue to trace the components of an air defense system down to electronic components or conceivably even to the atomic level. At some point, however, one ceases to be concerned with the structure of a component. At this point the component is treated as an elementary *black box* with known transformations between inputs and outputs but with unknown internal structure (Ashby, 1956, pp. 86–117).

No one person is concerned in detail with more than a very few hierarchical levels of a system. The complexity of a multilevel system soon gets out of hand, and so one must simply treat lower-level components as black boxes. Thus the project manager for an air defense system treats a computer as a black box, leaving to lower-level designers the task of specifying the internal structure of the computer.

That part of the world not included within a system's boundaries constitutes the *environment* of the system. For example, from the standpoint of the designer of a computer, the environment might be an air defense system of which the computer is a part. Interactions will, in general, exist between a system and its environment, but the *exogenous* variables

---

[3] Even with all this information, however, the complexity of the system may preclude an analytical determination of behavior. One must in this case resort to simulation techniques, which in principle can always be applied.

through which the interactions are manifested are treated as noncontrollable. Only the *endogenous* variables used to describe a system are considered to be subject to a significant degree of control.

The designation of an essentially arbitrary boundary between a system and its environment poses the danger that significant interactions will not be considered explicitly. Such failure introduces the penalty typically associated with *suboptimization*—the penalty of achieving local subgoals inconsistent with overall "global" goals (Hitch and McKean, 1960, pp. 128–131 and 158–181). For example, important interactions may exist between a computer and the associated communications equipment used in an air defense system. In specifying the interfaces and performance characteristics of individual items of equipment, the manager of the entire system attempts to reconcile conflicts between the designs of the computer and the communications equipment. Once these are set, however, the designers of the separate items of equipment must largely ignore the effects of their detailed decisions on other parts of the total system. This will not, in general, result in an "optimal" global design, but the complexity of the total task demands that it be approached in a relatively piecemeal fashion.

The internal structure of a system, like its boundary with the environment, is often arbitrary. Usually there exist a vast number of ways in which various detailed components of a system can be coalesced into a hierarchy of higher-level components. To be sure, not all structures are equally desirable. One tries to select a structure that combines interacting and complementary activities in a way that reduces interdependence among components and achieves efficiency in accomplishing the global objectives of the system.

Once a structure has been selected, it may impose severe constraints on the behavior of the system. For example, if certain functions are assigned to the communications subsystem in an air defense system, the system may behave differently than it would if the functions were assigned to the computer system. After a commitment is made to one structure, a change may entail substantial penalties.

1.3 *System Structure*

Alternative Structures

The question of system structure can be usefully pursued in some detail. Attention will be focused on man-made systems designed to achieve a given set of goals. A crucial design issue is the specification of the system's hierarchical structure. To be sure, structure is not the only critical specification, but it certainly is one of the more important ones.

The structure of a system results from breaking down, or *factoring,* its global goals into a hierarchy of less complex subsystems. This is done (often only implicitly) through a means–end analysis that relates the desired end result—the global goals—to the means of accomplishing them (March and Simon, 1958, pp. 151–154 and 190–193). Each subsystem presumably contributes to the accomplishment of the goals of its immediate higher-level system and therefore ultimately to the global goals. The process of factoring continues until the lowest-level subsystems are manageable without further breakdown.

The lowest-level subsystems at the end of each of the various means–end chains will be termed *elementary tasks.* They are elementary in the sense that they are viewed as *black boxes*—that is, their internal structure is not defined explicitly in terms of lower-level activities. An elementary task may, however, represent a fairly large subsystem—a chemical processing unit that performs a standard unit operation such as distillation, for example. Indeed, for some purposes an entire plant or division might be taken as an elementary task.

Let us make the somewhat artificial assumption that the set of elementary tasks is not affected by the way in which factoring takes place. In other words, the elementary tasks fully characterize the global task of the system, regardless of how they happen to be linked to each other and to the global activities.[4] To be sure, the efficiency with which the system carries on these activities depends greatly on its structure. It is the job of the systems designer to choose an efficient structure out of the vast set of alternative structures.

A systems designer necessarily limits the scope of the activities that he attempts to structure. He does this by arbitrarily considering certain clusters of activity as being black boxes, immune from internal structuring as far as he is concerned (at least for the time being). His job is therefore reduced to one of determining the hierarchical links among those subsystems he currently considers elemental.

---

[4] In the process of factoring global goals intermediate tasks govern the character of lower-level elementary tasks. Once the elementary tasks have been generated, they may be restructured in a way that alters the character of intermediate tasks. In an actual system, all tasks are likely to experience continual change through a process involving both the analysis of higher-level tasks and a synthesis from lower-level tasks.

The system structure describes the way in which the set of elementary tasks are hierarchically combined to form the complete system. Each structure represents a different system. For the sake of simplicity we shall limit the discussion to a particular (but common) type called a *tree structure*. A tree structure contains no cycles (that is, every subsystem is a component of only one higher-level subsystem), and all parts are connected together.[5] The "leaves" at the end of each branch of the tree represent elementary tasks of the system.

Even when we are limited to these special structures, a vast number of alternatives exist. As shown in Figure 1-1, with three identical elementary

(1)   (2)

Two Structures with Three Elementary Tasks

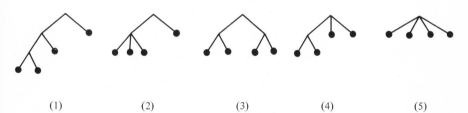

(1)   (2)   (3)   (4)   (5)

Five Structures with Four Elementary Tasks

Figure 1-1. Alternative structures with identical elementary tasks

tasks there are two different structures, and with four such tasks there are five alternatives. The number grows to a total of 2,312 alternative structures in the case of ten elementary tasks. With only fifty tasks, there are over 10^{24} alternatives. In an actual system most of the elementary tasks are, of course, distinct, rather than identical. This enormously expands the

---

[5] Such structures do not include all possibilities, of course. It may be very useful to design a system with a given subsystem serving as a component of several other subsystems. In a complex computer program, for example, the same subroutine may be used by several different subsystems. Even in organizations we find individuals serving simultaneously two different "bosses" (as in the so-called *matrix* organization, for example).

number of alternatives. For example, with three distinct elementary tasks there are four alternative structures, shown in Figure 1-2. With ten such tasks there are over 282 million alternatives, and with fifty distinct tasks the number swells to 6.85×10^{81} (Emery, 1965, p. 49).

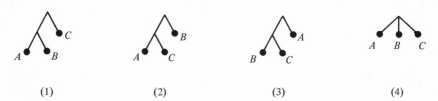

| (1) | (2) | (3) | (4) |

Figure 1-2. Alternative structures with three distinct elementary tasks

We need not be intimidated by this numbers game. A count of the alternative structures perhaps provides an interesting and impressive index of the impossible complexity of the systems problem facing a designer bent on finding an "optimal" structure. Paradoxically, the very vastness of the numbers simplifies the task of choosing a structure in practice.

As is typical of such combinatorial phenomena, the numbers grow far too rapidly in any practical problem for one to consider individually anything but a minute sample of available alternatives. As Bremermann (1962) and Ashby (1964) point out, physical laws forever bar us from dealing with as many as 10^{100} abstract objects, and, of course, the current state of technology places the upper limit many orders of magnitude below this figure. Thus the number of alternative structures is, from an operational standpoint, essentially infinite. The choice of a structure, therefore, cannot be made through a process of selecting from an exhaustive list of alternatives—just as a master chess move is not chosen from an exhaustive enumeration of alternative moves, and inspiring prose is not created by culling it out of an exhaustive list of alphabetic character strings. In such cases, we must rely essentially on multistage processes in which each stage reduces combinatorially the number of remaining alternatives to be considered. We can cope with combinatorial growth only with equally powerful combinatorial elimination.

Characteristics of Alternative Structures

Before discussing the design process let us first examine some of the important characteristics of alternative structures. These characteristics have an important bearing on the relative effectiveness of each alternative.

Degree of Fragmentation of the System.   Hierarchical fragmentation of the system invariably leaves interactions among its parts.[6] But fragmentation also imposes barriers to coordination across the boundaries separating the various parts of the system. Fragmentation thus simplifies the system by creating relatively isolated subsystems, but it does this at the cost of introducing communications barriers among interacting activities. These barriers typically carry a penalty of suboptimization and may lead to un-desirable dynamic behavior (Forrester, 1961, pp. 183–185 and 329–335).

The definition of fragmentation can be made more precise. Fragmenta-tion occurs when a task is separated into two or more subtasks. Each frag-ment created may, in turn, be further fragmented. The total fragmentation of a system can be measured by the number of nodes in its tree structure; these represent the nonelementary tasks created by the factoring process. Figure 1-3 shows the fragmentation, f, of different structures with eight elementary tasks. It can be shown (Emery, 1965, pp. 52–53) that the fragmentation of a structure equals $(n - 1)/(s - 1)$, where n is the num-ber of elementary tasks and s is the average *span* at each node (that is, the number of tasks directly comprising a higher-level task—eight in part 1 of Figure 1-3 and two in part 3).

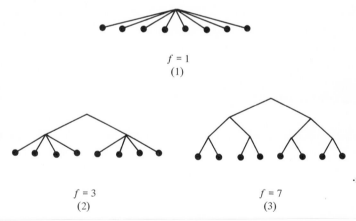

$f = 1$
(1)

$f = 3$ $f = 7$
(2)   (3)

Figure 1-3. Fragmentation, f, of three different structures having eight elementary functions

Thus the fragmentation of a structure is inversely related to span. The maximum fragmentation obviously occurs when s equals 2. In this case, $f = n - 1$, and there exist virtually as many fragments as elementary tasks.

[6] If this were not the case, each independent fragment would essentially represent a separate system. But the *sine qua non* of a system is the interdependence of its parts.

The minimum fragmentation occurs when s equals n, and hence only one "fragment" exists—that is, the entire system. This unfragmented structure has a completely flat hierarchical structure and therefore eliminates the problems introduced by interaction among lower-level fragments.[7]

Complexity of Subsystem Tasks.   The ubiquity of multi-level hierarchical structures testifies to their usefulness. The relative isolation of each fragment of the system drastically reduces the number of relationships that must be considered in coping with the tasks assigned to a subsystem. Although ignoring activities in other portions of the system leads to suboptimization, the complexity of the total system task leaves no other choice. Suboptimization is the price of feasibility.

Let us consider the effect of structure on the complexity of a subsystem task. The number of potential relationships among immediate lower-level tasks provides a rough index of the relative complexity of a higher-level task.[8] The total number of different subsets of a set with n objects is 2^n (including the empty set). Therefore, in the absence of fragmentation, a system with n elementary tasks involves $2^n - 1$ relationships.

With fragmentation, a subsystem must deal in detail with only those tasks directly composing it. If a span of s is used, the number of potential relationships is reduced from $2^n - 1$ to $2^s - 1$. (Graicunas [1937] gives this same formula.) Since s is normally very much smaller than n, the effect is to reduce a patently infeasible problem to a manageable one.

The number of potential relationships is very sensitive to the value of s: an increase of one in the span roughly doubles the number of relationships. As we have seen earlier, fragmentation is inversely related to s. Ideally, one would like to set s at a value that balances the costs of fragmentation against the cost of coping with a large number of interacting subtasks.

The balance point depends, of course, on the nature of the tasks being performed. If strong interactions exist (and are not ignored), the span

---

[7] It should be noted that a completely flat hierarchical structure having a span of n is not the same as a nonhierarchical structure. In the former, there exists a top-level system responsible for coordinating the actions of the n elementary tasks. A completely nonhierarchical disconnected structure, on the other hand, is essentially anarchic.

[8] These are obviously not the only relationships that must be taken into account; relationships with other subsystems must also be considered. However, only the number of relationships among a subsystem's own immediate components changes as a function of its own structure, and therefore the number of relationships gives a *relative* measure of task complexity as it is affected by internal structure.

must be kept narrow in order to keep the tasks manageable. If tasks involve relatively weak interactions, the span can be increased considerably without unduly increasing task complexity.

It is hazardous to generalize further about the ideal span. Its determination involves an exceedingly complex tradeoff between fragmentation and coordination. The tradeoff depends critically on the number and variety of tasks being coordinated, the degree of interaction among the tasks, and the data-handling capacity available for coordination. All one can say with some assurance is that the human mind has fairly stringent limits on its information-handling capacity (Miller, 1956), and so the span must be quite narrow if a human coordinator is expected to take into account detailed internal or external interactions.

Communications Within the System. Coordination of a system requires communication among its parts. In the face of ever-present interactions, the "optimal" behavior of any given subsystem depends on the activities of other subsystems. Communication channels are therefore required to provide information about such activities.

As many others have pointed out (for example, Simon, 1960, pp. 41–42), direct communication between all subsystems is clearly out of the question in a system of even moderate size. In a nonhierarchical system, there exist $\frac{1}{2}n(n-1)$ pairs of direct links. In a hierarchical system, if direct channels are established between all tasks (both elementary and nonelementary), the number of links is increased by a factor of nearly $\left(\frac{s}{s-1}\right)^2$. In either case, the number of information channels is of the order of n^2—a very large number indeed for any reasonably sized system.

Hierarchical communication channels—as opposed to direct ones—greatly reduce both the number of total links in the network and the number of links that each separate subsystem must maintain. In a structure having a uniform span of s, each node has s direct links with lower-level tasks. Since there are $(n-1)/(s-1)$ nodes, the structure consists of a *total* of $(n-1) \cdot \left(\frac{s}{s-1}\right)$ communication links. Thus the number of links grows in proportion to the number of elementary functions, rather than the square of this number.

A price must be paid for this economy, however. Except in the case of communication between a node and its immediate subordinate tasks, all coordination in a purely hierarchical communication network takes place through one or more intervening nodes. Each node tends to introduce delays and distortion in the messages passing through it. The average number of intervening nodes through which messages pass in a hierarchical network with uniform span is approximately $2 \cdot \log_s n - 4/(s - 1) - 1$ (Emery, 1965, pp. 81–85). Although this figure grows at a very much lower rate than n, in a large system the number of intervening nodes is large enough to impede seriously the flow of information among subsystems.[9]

Because of the "distance" separating tasks along hierarchical links, the information network of a system typically includes a number of important direct links between closely coupled activities. In fact, the bulk of routine coordination may be of this form—when, for example, sales orders flow from a remote sales office directly to the accounting, production, and engineering departments.

Supplementary direct links offer both the advantages and disadvantages of direct communication: they eliminate some of the distortion and delays caused by a series of intervening nodes, but can also result in an unwieldy proliferation of information channels. Fortunately, a given task typically interacts closely with only a few other activities, and so the need for specialized direct links is fairly limited. Moreover, such links typically deal with routine activities and therefore they can be handled largely through standard procedures that provide programmed coordination.

Often a more attractive alternative is to superimpose over the hierarchical channels an information system that links each task to a common information pool, or *data base*.[10] Such a system is illustrated in Figure 1-4. This network offers both economy in information channels and a relatively close linkage between every pair of activities.

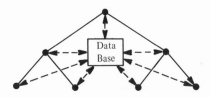

Figure 1-4. Information channels with
a common data base

[9] It is interesting to observe that the *average* number of intervening nodes is not very different from the *maximum* number of $2 \cdot \log_s n$ that separates two elementary tasks in different first-level branches of the tree. Thus, most tasks are relatively "distant" from all other tasks.

[10] The data base consists of all formal (and normally machine-readable) information available within the organization.

Criteria for Choosing a Structure

As we have seen, the systems designer has a vast—effectively infinite —number of alternative structures from which to choose. Each structure has certain important characteristics that affect its suitability, such as the number and complexity of subsystems and the efficiency of communication among them. From the available alternatives the designer must choose a suitable structure. Various criteria provide rather ill-defined heuristics for making this choice.

Information-Handling Requirements. Limitations on information handling impose severe restrictions on the choice of structure. In the absence of such limitations, the designer should choose the structure having the least fragmentation and fewest channels of communication—namely, the structure with a span of n and depth of one. But this structure would normally place an impossible information-handling burden on the single coordinating node, and therefore the designer must choose a structure with much more modest computation requirements.

The information-handling required at a given node depends on the nature and number of subtasks and the type of higher-level constraints imposed. An increase in the number of tasks coordinated, or an increase in the degree of interaction among them, adds to computational requirements. On the other hand, a higher-level constraint may either increase or decrease lower-level information-handling requirements. For example, a constraint that calls for specific actions (or bars specific actions) reduces the set of alternatives that must be examined. But a constraint on performance that does not specify how the desired result is to be achieved may increase information-processing requirements by triggering an expanded search for an alternative that satisfies the constraint.

Because of these complexities, one cannot generalize much about the way in which information-handling limitations restrict the choice of alternative structures. However, if we use span as a grossly simplified index of processing requirements, it is possible to show the effect of these limitations.

A span of less than a prescribed lower bound can be ruled out as causing excessive fragmentation. Similarly, the designer can also eliminate from consideration those structures that include a span that exceeds an upper bound corresponding to the limits on information handling. Such bounds dramatically slash the number of alternative structures.

For example, if spans are restricted to the range of from 5 to 10, the number of permitted alternatives with 50 distinct elementary functions drops from 6.8×10^{81} to 1.2×10^{51}—a reduction factor of better than 10^{30}. Although the remaining number of alternatives is obviously beyond any exhaustive analysis, these figures do illustrate the effectiveness of such restrictions in reducing the number of alternatives. The heuristics used in selecting a structure consist essentially of imposing such restrictions that eliminate from consideration those alternatives that appear to have a low probability of falling within an acceptable range of information-handling requirements.

Interaction Among Activities. The activities combined under a given node are normally closely interacting. There are two primary reasons for this: such a structure facilitates communications, and it simplifies the task of coping with interactions.

As we have seen, most pairs of subsystems are separated by a relatively large number of hierarchical nodes. Although usually some direct communication channels exist, hierarchical links nevertheless provide an important channel of coordination, particularly for nonroutine matters.[11] If closely interacting tasks are clustered together, the average hierarchical path along which information must flow will be greatly reduced. On the other hand, weakly interacting tasks can be made quite "distant," since very little communication takes place between such activities.

An even greater advantage of combining closely related tasks is that it permits a more rational handling of interactions. Limited information-handling capacity severely restricts the number of tasks that can be co-ordinated in detail. It is therefore advantageous to combine strongly interacting tasks so that their interactions can be coped with within this limit. Only minor penalties result from ignoring interactions with the less closely related tasks.

Complementarity Among Activities. Two or more tasks are complementary when they can be performed jointly more efficiently than separately. Complementarities may arise through the discreteness of the resources required by separate tasks, the existence of economies of scale, or the inherently joint nature of the technology employed. For example, two research activities exhibit complementarity if they both require part-time use of an expensive item of equipment or a highly specialized scientist. Similarly, two complementary components of a computer may use the same power source. Data-processing tasks usually show marked complementarity,

[11] Routine coordination between interacting but "distant" subunits can be handled through specialized links and programmed procedures.

since combining activities provides pronounced economies of scale in computation.

The degree to which a given structure permits the exploitation of such complementarities is an important criterion in judging its suitability. On the other hand, combining complementary activities creates—or, rather, explicitly recognizes—additional interactions. For example, if two tasks use the same specialized resources, interactions arise through the allocation of the common resource. If these tasks were organized as separate subsystems, each with its own individual resource, no interactions would exist.

Consistency of Assignable Goals with Higher-Level Goals.   The fact that a system is fragmented into a hierarchy of subsystems implies that each of the resulting fragmented tasks is partially independent of all other tasks. Designers of higher-level subsystems attempt to achieve lower-level purposeful behavior (that is, behavior consistent with higher-level goals) by imposing various goals and constraints on lower-level subsystems. The effectiveness of a given cluster of lower-level tasks is therefore governed in part by the ability of higher-level designers to assign reasonable constraints that lead to desirable behavior.

Take the business organization as an illustration of this concept. A desire to establish "profit centers" provides for many business firms a strong motivation to bring together all those activities that can be identified with a single profit-generating activity. Often the fragmentation of the organization is by major product lines, with each profit center operating all of the activities associated with a given product line. Each of the profit centers can then be assigned a relatively sparse set of goals—namely, the goals typically thought to motivate any private business, such as accounting profit, rate of growth, and share of market.[12]

In an organization fragmented instead by, say, functional activities— sales, engineering, and manufacturing, for example—a suitable measure of performance may not be so apparent. In the face of strong interactions that normally exist among functions, a sparse set of goals may simply not provide sufficient information to lower-level units to motivate them to behave in a way consistent with higher-level goals. Under these circumstances rela-

---

[12] It should be pointed out, however, that the simplicity and usefulness of such a profit figure may often be largely illusory, since interactions among products must be handled through such mechanisms as arbitrary transfer prices and cost allocations. Nevertheless, a profit measure has great appeal for managers anxious to boil down all performance into a single index. A good summary of the issues involved is contained in Gordon (1964).

tively abundant constraints must be imposed. For example, in order to handle interactions between sales and manufacturing, it might be necessary to constrain schedules, quality, product mix, and the like. Such centralized direction may have a number of advantages, but parsimony in the amount of information transmitted among activities is not one of them.

Design of System Structure

"Optimizing" Structure.   The design of a system is much more an art than a science. The procedures for determining the fragmentation of the total system are embodied in rather vague *heuristics* (or "rules of thumb") rather than well-defined rules. Some optimizing procedures have been developed, but these have had very little general applicability.

Alexander (1964) has made an interesting attempt to develop an algorithm for systems synthesis. He is specifically interested in problems of architectural design, but strong similarities exist between the design of, say, an Indian village (Alexander, 1964, pp. 136–173) and any other system.

The first step in his procedure is the specification of a set of design requirements (corresponding to elementary tasks). For example, in the design for a village there exists the requirement that all parts of the village have convenient access to bus transportation. This set of requirements is generated through an analysis of the overall objectives of the design.

Next, the interaction between each pair of requirements is determined. Interaction is measured in terms of a correlation-like index that specifies the degree to which the satisfaction of one of the requirements affects the satisfaction of the other member of the pair. If the index is positive, the requirements are complementary. This is true, for example, of the requirements that a building have good thermal insulation and a low noise level from external sources. A negative index indicates that the achievement of one requirement makes it more difficult to achieve the other—the requirements that a building be both inexpensive and earthquake proof, for example.

Alexander has developed a means for partitioning these requirements into a hierarchy of subsets such that the interactions across subsets are minimized. Each of the subsets, consisting of strongly interacting requirements, can then be tackled as a relatively independent design problem. Since interaction with the other design problems is weak, hopefully the solutions to all such subproblems will constitute a satisfactory solution to the entire problem. If, on the contrary, strong interactions existed among subproblems, each separate solution might have to be altered significantly in the process of meshing all solutions together.

Unfortunately, the assumptions made in order to simplify the mathematics make the procedure far from general (Alexander, 1964, pp. 112–113). For one thing, the mere identification of elementary tasks is usually quite difficult. These tasks are generated, at least in part, through an analysis of higher-level systems (see page 6). Even if elementary tasks have been identified, Alexander's procedure is limited by the fact that only pairwise interactions are allowed; interactions among three or more requirements are assumed to be negligible. But in the design of most systems, these higher-order interactions can be of decisive importance. For example, the interaction among the fabrication, assembly, and shipping departments in a factory cannot be described simply in terms of the interactions between the three possible pairs of departments.

Such attempts to develop optimizing procedures for systems design shed light on the problems involved, but as yet offer little more than this. The objective function to be optimized is typically so ill-defined as to defy attempts to express it in explicit form. Even measuring some of the important variables involved, such as the degree of interaction among activities, presents an extremely formidable problem.

Heuristics for Determining Structure.   Although the development of a general optimizing procedure for structural design seems well beyond our present capability, this is hardly an excuse for inaction. Somehow the structure *does* get established. In choosing a structure the designer must rely on rough heuristics.[13]

A description of good systems-design methodology is really a description of problem solving. It seems quite clear that the human mind is incapable of dealing at one time with more than a handful of interacting variables (Miller, 1956). In dealing with problems having many such variables, the human gets around his limited information-processing capability by factoring the problem into a hierarchy of subproblems (Newell, Shaw, and Simon, 1959).

And so it is in designing a complex system. The process involves the solution of a series of local subproblems that have been identified provisionally through the factoring of higher-level problems. The higher- and lower-level aspects of a problem then enter only in aggregate terms (if at all). Once a local subproblem is solved, it subsequently enters into other subproblems in a similar aggregate fashion.

The design process thus becomes one of nibbling away on the global problem. Under these circumstances, it is difficult to separate the analysis

---

[13] Goetz (1949, pp. 76–83) illustrates such heuristics applied to the design of an organizational structure.

from the synthesis stage of the process. The local problem is made small enough that the human mind can cope with the two stages simultaneously. Confined to a local problem, one can begin to contemplate an exhaustive search of alternatives. Repeated local searches of this type hopefully converge on a satisfactory solution of the global problem.

Let us consider an example that illustrates the efficiency of this search process. Suppose that we have identified (through a previous problem-solving process) fifty distinct elementary tasks that we wish to combine in some satisfactory way. As seen earlier, there are over 10^{81} different ways of structuring these fifty tasks. But suppose it is possible to identify a cluster of, say, five tasks that clearly must be organized so that they are hierarchically close. The activities may, for example, exhibit especially strong interactions or complementarities.

Now, among five distinct elementary tasks there are only 236 different possible structures. An exhaustive evaluation of these alternatives may be perfectly feasible. If not, relatively simple heuristics can ordinarily be found to dismiss out of hand the obviously poor alternatives. In any case, let us assume that the designer can determine a satisfactory structure among the five clustered tasks. From the standpoint of the other tasks, then, the five tasks have been collapsed into a single (composite) task. As a result, there now exist only forty-six tasks—the consolidated task and the forty-five remaining tasks.

This process can be continued. If each repetition compresses five tasks into a single composite task, a total of thirteen cycles will be required. Each cycle requires an evaluation of 236 alternative structures, except the last, which involves only two tasks (and hence permits only a single structure). Therefore, a total of only 2,832 alternatives must be evaluated (instead of 10^{81}).

To be sure, the suitability of the resulting structure depends critically on whether the tasks grouped together should, in fact, be so clustered. By its very nature, the choice of clustered activities constrains the final structure to one that contains those particular groupings.

The larger the cluster of tasks selected for exhaustive research, the less severe the constraint and hence the better the final structure. However, an analysis of larger clusters obviously expands the number of alternatives to be evaluated. For example, if clusters of eight tasks are consolidated in every iteration, an exhaustive evaluation must deal with a total of over four million alternatives. Thus, whether exhaustive or not, the job of evaluation is very much more difficult than when clusters are limited to five tasks (but obviously much *less* difficult than the case in which no clusters are formed).

Despite the (nonoptimal) constraints imposed by the clustering procedure, it offers a very powerful method of searching for improved structures. Any systems designer confronted by a virtually infinite variety of alternatives undoubtedly employs a "pruning" heuristic of this sort. And within a larger cluster he probably forms subclusters to prune the problem still further. If he makes a reasonably suitable choice of clusters, the final structure may not be too far from the optimum.

In any case, the choice of structure is usually not final. The system must go through a continual process of learning and adaptation. Change of structure is one means of effecting this adaptation. Such changes are necessarily of a rather local nature—that is, they involve the rearrangement of relatively few tasks (Morris, 1968, pp. 11–14). But even local improvements can in time effect profound changes.[14]

---

[14] Strictly local changes can, in general, never lead to a global optimum, however. A system that has evolved along given lines finds only a relatively small number of new structures accessible to it through local adaptation. Because of this, it may not be able to find even a *stable* structure (let alone the optimal one) in the face of a changed environment—to which the dinosaurs bear mute testimony.

CHAPTER 2

The Organization As a System

ALTHOUGH conceptually the design process is much the same for all systems, it nevertheless will be fruitful to concentrate primarily on a particular type of system, the organization. There are two reasons for this. First, a book on planning and control is naturally concerned with the special characteristics of the organization. Second, there is some value in using concrete, well-known examples even when discussing general abstract properties of systems.

2.1 The Hierarchical Structure of Organizations

The hierarchical nature of organizations is, of course, well known. Every beginning text in organization theory stresses this characteristic. For the most part, hierarchy is viewed as an authority relationship. For example, a foreman has a subordinate hierarchical role in relation to the plant superintendent because the superintendent "bosses" the foreman.

The hierarchical character of organizations stems from deeper roots than mere authority relationships; it stems, rather, from the need to reduce the apparent complexity of the system. Organizations, like all systems, have a hierarchical structure that results from factoring global objectives into a hierarchy of more manageable subobjectives. What we view as organizational structure—the compartmentalization of the organization's resources, the authority to direct the use of these resources, and the responsibility for achieving assigned objectives—represents an effort to implement the results of the factoring process.

The behavior of the organization rests largely on the way in which the factoring is accomplished. Fragmentation of the organization's global objectives into a hierarchy of subobjectives inevitably introduces problems of coordination. It is therefore desirable to make each subactivity as comprehensive as the information-handling capacity of the organization allows.

Authority relationships are, of course, closely related to the hierarchical structure of an organization. Since the success of any organizational unit in meeting its assigned responsibilities depends on the composite performance of its subunits, the higher-level unit must have some authority to direct the behavior of the lower-level units. Typically, this authority vests in higher-level managers the power to specify lower-level goals, to allocate resources (including managerial resources) among lower-level subunits, and, on occasions, to change its organizational structure.[1]

2.2 *Interactions Among Organizational Subunits*

In order to reap the benefit of the simplifications introduced by the factoring process, each organizational unit must be largely isolated from the rest. Without partial independence, each unit would require access to detailed information about all other activities with which it interacts. In effect, each unit would have to handle the global problem.

Sources of Interactions

Despite the need for independence, interactions among activities are a fact of life. They exist almost universally and are the prime source of the conflict that exists among organizational subunits. They are manifested in three fundamental ways.

[1] The way in which this power is used varies greatly among organizations and individual managers. In an authoritarian organization the power is exercised openly and explicitly. In an organization run along more participative lines the power may exit only in latent form, resorted to openly only if negotiation and coaxing fail. Nevertheless, some higher-level authority must be available to resolve the conflicts that inevitably arise among organizational subunits.

First, interactions occur as a result of *coupling* between units through their inputs and outputs. The factoring process nearly always fragments the activities connected with the transformation of material, energy, and information. Consequently, each unit, in carrying on its own subactivity, must typically rely on other units to perform their assigned part of a common higher-level activity. For example, a given process in a chemical plant may rely on other units to supply necessary intermediate materials, power, and steam.

The couplings may be of different types. *Serial* coupling represents the simplest case. Here unit A is coupled serially with unit B which in turn is coupled to unit $C:$

$$A \longrightarrow B \longrightarrow C$$

Parallel coupling exists when one unit is coupled to two or more other units:

$$A \underset{\longrightarrow C}{\overset{\longrightarrow B}{\rule{2cm}{0pt}}}$$

Feedback coupling arises when "loops" occur—when, for example, unit A is coupled with unit B, which is then coupled back to unit $A:$

$$\rightarrow A \longrightarrow B$$

The preceding diagram illustrates direct or "immediate" feedback coupling (Ashby, 1956, p. 57). Indirect or "ultimate" feedback coupling occurs when the feedback loop includes three or more components, as in the following diagram:

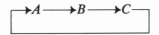

In practice, of course, all types of coupling may occur simultaneously. In a large organization, the links among subunits typically form an exceedingly elaborate network.

A second (but related) way in which interactions are transmitted is through a common environment. In other words, all coupling need not be internal to the system. For example, one product department of a decentralized company may engage in practices that harm the reputation of the entire company, affecting the sales of all other departments. External agents such as customers, labor unions, competitors, and the government can all serve as channels for transmitting interactions among organizational units.[2]

Finally, some interactions stem from the allocation of scarce common resources. All types of resources (managerial talent, labor, materials, energy, capital equipment, and funds[3]) are subject to limitation, at least in the short run. Consequently, the assignment of resources to one unit affects the allocation of resources to all other units. This source of interaction does not require any coupling of organizational units; even highly "independent" activities may draw upon the same pool of overall resources.

Means of Reducing Interactions

In the presence of interactions, each decision made within one subunit can have almost endless ramifications throughout the rest of the organization. An attempt to trace all such effects would place an intolerable burden on the information-handling capacity of the organization. In order to cope with this problem, the organization resorts to various devices that drastically reduce the coordination required among subunits.

Organization Structure.   As discussed in the previous chapter, organizational structure has a major effect on the degree of interaction among subunits. Interactions can be reduced greatly by structuring the organization so that closely related activities are hierarchically "near" to each other. Conversely, weakly interacting activities are normally structured so that they are hierarchically "distant" from each other in order to conserve the relatively few close links that each subunit can maintain with other units.

Unfortunately, this principle is often difficult to apply in practice. An organizational structure that reduces one type of interaction may increase another. For example, a *project* (or *purpose*) organizational structure in its purest form assigns to a single branch of the hierarchy all of the tasks, and only those tasks, connected with an independent objective. This provides a high degree of independence, and thus reduces the amount of coordination required among subunits.

---

[2] Defining a coupling agent as external to the system is essentially an arbitrary question. If the coupling is strong enough, considerable distortion may result by not treating the agent as part of the system. See Section 1.2.

[3] Each of these can, of course, be classified into more specialized resources, such as lathes or lathe operators.

Alternatively, a *functional* (or *process*) organizational structure combines elementary activities that serve multiple purposes—all of the electrical engineering work associated with several different development projects, for instance. By recognizing the interaction among activities caused by the use of a common resource (electrical engineers), the organization can achieve greater specialization and increased utilization of resources. The considerable attendant efficiencies of consolidation may be gained, however, at the cost of assigning closely interacting tasks to different subunits (for example, the designing of a complex electromechanical device might be split between the electrical and mechanical engineering departments). A functional structure may therefore greatly increase the volume of information that must be transmitted among subunits in the course of coordinating their efforts.

In practice, of course, organizations invariably resort to a combination of purpose and process structures. For instance, an organization structured at its highest level by purpose is likely to be structured at the next level by process. The so-called "matrix" organization is the most explicit example of a combined structure. Although the purpose form seems to be enjoying increasing favor, particularly in the management of large research and development projects, the correct balance between the two forms depends on the particular (and often changing) circumstances facing the organization.

Decoupling.   The amount of coordination required among subunits is by no means fixed solely by the choice of a given structure; the degree of coordination required is also governed by other decisions. The use of various *decoupling* devices offers one of the primary ways of reducing the need for coordination (March and Simon, 1958, pp. 158–160). These devices increase short-term independence among subunits by mitigating the effects of coupling.

Decoupling can be achieved by limiting the number of input–output couplings that constitute the explicit interfaces among subunits. Because of the highly interdependent nature of most organizations, each subunit has a staggering number of potential interfaces. Tracing the detailed ramifications of every action obviously represents an impossible task, so the organization must severely limit the number of the interfaces that a subunit considers in carrying on its own activities. The "significant" links are treated as interfaces, while the vast bulk of them are ignored or aggregated with other interfacing variables.

For example, a production planner may schedule his department without detailed consideration of the effects of his actions on others. He relies on other planners to cope within their own departments with such unfavorable effects as varying labor requirements, machine capacity limitations, and shortages of raw materials. He thus artificially isolates himself to a considerable extent by generating suboptimal plans based on the fiction that most of the interactions with the other departments do not exist. Hopefully, such suboptimization represents a legitimate and useful simplification of reality.

Often the severing of a given interface is not complete, but is instead conditional upon existing conditions. Under this scheme, coordination among units need not take place unless an interface variable falls outside of established threshold limits. As Ashby points out (1956, p. 66), "the existence of thresholds induces a state of affairs that can be regarded as a cutting of the whole into temporary isolated subsystems; for a variable, so long as it stays constant, cannot . . . have an effect on another; neither can it be affected by another." Typically, relatively minor variations account for the bulk of deviations, and therefore a truncation of this portion of the random distribution drastically reduces the volume of interunit communications. Like the compartmentalization of a ship by means of watertight bulkheads, interface thresholds provide a partial barrier to the transmission of random effects from one part of the organization to another and allow each part to carry on its activities in relative isolation. Figure 2–1 illustrates this concept.

Numerous illustrations can be cited of the use of interface thresholds. The "exception" principle, which restricts communication to those variables outside their control limits, provides a common example. Often lower-level

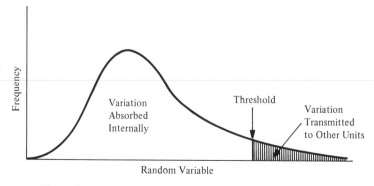

Figure 2-1. The cushioning effect of an interface threshold

managers are granted discretionary authority over matters that fall below some threshold of importance (such as the expenditure of funds for minor repairs or capital projects).

Standardization of interfaces represent another means of decoupling. The specification of the standard characteristics of an input or output, in terms of such variables as the mean and allowed range of its various characteristics, reduces the need for communication among subunits.

For instance, if one part of the organization supplies another part with an input material, the supplying unit must meet certain specifications. An intermediate chemical, say, may have an allowed range for specific gravity and a maximum limit on iron and sulfur content. The receiving subunit can thus engage in its own activities on the assumption that the supplying unit will meet the specified requirements. The supplying unit is expected to absorb most random variations that occur in its own process in order to insulate other parts of the organization from the effects of these variations.

Similar standard specifications may be established for information inputs and outputs. Organizations often employ standard identification codes to reduce problems of coordination. Standardization of such characteristics as data formats, frequencies, and allowed time lags permits the independent implementation of various parts of an information system as long as the specified interfaces are not affected.

Accounting standards can be thought of as a means of decoupling. For example, a maintenance department may charge at a standard rate for each of its services, regardless of the "actual" cost of providing them. In this way, variations in the efficiency of maintenance are not transmitted to the users.

Another means of partially decoupling organizational units is through the use of *buffers*. A buffer provides intermediate storage capacity for the inputs and outputs flowing among subunits. Without such buffers, the output rate of a supplying unit would have to match exactly the input rate of a receiving unit, necessitating very close coordination. With buffers, short-term differences between input and output rates can be cushioned through fluctuations in the level of buffer inventories. Consequently, variation between input and output rates need not involve coordination as long as the cumulative deviation falls within prescribed limits (for example, limits set by buffer capacity or by the need to maintain minimum inventory levels).

The best-known examples of buffers are those involving physical inventories of materials. Buffer inventory almost invariably exists between supplying and using departments. Even in the case of feeder departments connected to the assembly department through a system of conveyers, some variation is normally allowed in the in-transit "float" inventory. Very much larger buffer stocks are usually provided in the case of discontinuous processes. In a multilevel physical distribution system, buffer inventories exist at each level.

Buffers are also used to cushion the flow of information inputs and outputs. A message center, for example, must have available buffer areas in order to provide temporary storage for messages waiting to be processed or relayed to some other point.

Still another method of obtaining partial decoupling is through the use of flexible resources within each subunit. Without flexibility, each subunit is likely to be extremely sensitive to random shocks, and a slight deviation from plans may cascade into larger and larger deviations. Under these circumstances, it is very difficult to predict the behavior of each subunit very far in advance.

Flexibility changes this picture. It allows each subunit to absorb minor random disturbances so that they are not propagated very far from their source. The behavior of each subunit thus becomes much more predictable. As a result, plans can be formulated over a longer time span. Coordination therefore requires relatively infrequent communication among the subunits, rather than a constant stream of information telling one part of the organization what is happening in other parts.

Flexibility can be achieved fundamentally in two different ways. First, the organization can employ flexible or "general-purpose" resources, such as digital-controlled machine tools and workers who are skilled in operating several types of machine. Such flexibility has the effect of increasing the number of activities that employ a given class of resource. Aggregate resource requirements can be predicted with greater relative accuracy than can the requirement for a smaller subset of the activities, since aggregation increases the likelihood that compensating errors will occur.[4]

Flexibility can also be achieved through the use of excess, or "slack," resources and time. A good schedule is not one that loads the shop at 100 per cent "efficiency," but rather one that leaves some extra capacity available in order to allow for the inevitable fluctuations in resource requirements. Similarly, a good schedule recognizes interactions among individual tasks by allowing excess time for each task. For example, a job that involves only ten hours of actual work may require a scheduled time of

---

[4] If the individual activities are statistically independent, the variance of the prediction of total resource requirements equals the sum of the variances of individual predictions. It can be shown that the standard deviation of the total is therefore less than the sum of individual standard deviations.

forty hours in order to compensate for the time it sits idle waiting to be assigned to an available machine. An "optimal" schedule is thus not a perfectly "efficient" one, since it takes into account not only the cost of direct resources but also the resources used for coordination.[5]

2.3 *Coordination Among Subunits*

Handling Interactions Through Coordination

The organization has still another means of coping with interactions— namely, the coordination of interacting activities through the transmission of information among subunits. Each subunit receives information that describes its own required actions as well as the anticipated actions of other subunits. This information is designed to induce each subunit to behave in a way that is consistent with the global objectives of the organization and with the activities of other parts of the organization.

Coordination is achieved principally through plans. Higher-level plans are transmitted throughout the organization as a means of directing be- havior on the part of lower-level subunits. They are designed to make the organization behave as a coordinated, goal-directed system, rather than as a loose collection of undisciplined parts. They reflect the factoring of the organization's global objectives into a hierarchy of subobjectives. Each level in the hierarchy generates plans for its lower-level units that are consistent with its own goals and constraints.

Plans should recognize various types of interactions among subunits. For example, the scheduled production of two physically coupled subunits should be set by a higher-level authority in a way that takes into account existing coupling relationships and the current level of buffer inventories. External interactions can be handled by such means as the specification of common policies affecting customers, workers, and the government.

Interactions arising from the allocation of scarce common resources necessarily require higher-level resolution. The resulting allocation deci- sions are communicated in the form of plans. A plan may specify an explicit allocation of a given resource to each lower-level activity, such as a capital budget that allocates specified amounts of funds to given projects or organizational units. Alternatively, resource rationing may be affected through the specification of procedures for analyzing potential applications of resources in a way that ensures that total resource constraints are not

---

[5] Queueing models demonstrate that queues grow indefinitely long as scheduled resource utilization approaches 100 per cent.

violated (analogous to the use of shadow prices or Lagrangian multipliers in constrained optimization problems).

A plan does not spring full-blown from the mind of a higher-level manager. It often represents a consensus of those it directs. A budget, for example, may flow downward through an organization, but it is based on information that has come from outside the organization or has previously flowed upward from the directed subunits. Primitive data of this sort provide the raw material for the generation of plans and thus play a vital role in the coordination of the organization.

Primitive data furnish the organization with a view of the world. This view may be subject to errors, delays, biases, filtering, and all sorts of other distortions, but the organization has no choice but to rely on it. The generation of plans depends not on any objective reality but largely on the description of reality provided by primitive data.[6] Therefore, the characteristics of such data—their sources, the transformations (both intended and otherwise) used to generate them, and their recipients—have a profound effect on the behavior of the organization.

Tradeoff Between Coordination and Independence

We have seen that the organization can increase the independence of its components by a suitable choice of organizational structure and the use of various decoupling devices. The limiting case of this approach—a system whose components are completely independent—is called a *completely decomposable* system[7] (Simon and Ando, 1961, pp. 114–115; Ando and Fisher, 1963). Such a system requires no coordination among its independent subsystems. Each subsystem carries on its own activities aimed at accomplishing its own independent objectives. The behavior of the total system is merely the composite behavior of the separate subsystems.

No organization achieves such complete isolation of its components; significant interactions persist despite all efforts to reduce them. At the very least, the components share common resources and global objectives. Given these inevitable interactions, an attempt to achieve a high degree of independence carries a heavy price.

---

[6] An executive's reliance on information available from a formal system or reported by others, instead of from firsthand observations, depends on the size of the organization. The larger the organization, the more dependent he becomes on secondhand information.

[7] It is debatable whether a completely decomposable system can usefully be considered a system at all. Operationally, it is merely a collection of independent systems.

For example, suboptimization achieved by ignoring interactions carries some well-known (but often overlooked) penalties. A schedule that appears attractive to the assembly section may, for instance, cause extreme bottlenecks in some of the subassembly departments. An obvious need exists for coordinating the activities of separate subunits in a way that recognizes such effects.

Other means of achieving independence also involve costs of various kinds: Combining related activities may result in forgone opportunities for greater specialization. Thresholds may screen out significant information. Tighter tolerances designed to increase the standardization of interfaces almost always increase the cost of producing the interfacing outputs. Buffer inventories take money to acquire and maintain. General-purpose resources typically cost more than special-purpose ones. And slack resources reduce capital and labor utilization.

Thus, complete independence is impossible to attain and very expensive to approach. In the absence of such independence, the organization must coordinate the activities of its subunits. But this, too, carries a price. The price takes the form of the resources employed in processing the information used for coordination: its collection, transmission, storage, computation, and display. Sometimes even more significant are the costs of designing and implementing the information system and the human decision making required to operate it. Finally, coordination inevitably introduces some degree of centralization of decision making, with its cost of delays, inflexibilities, and loss of information about local needs and local conditions (Goode and Machol, 1957, p. 317). In short, as the organization attempts to trace more and more of the detailed ramifications of interactions, the costs of coordination climb very steeply indeed.

The organization is thus confronted with a problem of tradeoffs. It must try to strike a balance between the costs of achieving greater independence and the costs of coordination. Figure 2-2 illustrates the principle involved. The horizontal axis measures the degree of coordination. At the left, complete independence exists among organizational units, and therefore no coordination is required. Coordination increases as the organization moves to the right along the axis. Complete coordination is achieved when the organization's activities are managed as a single monolithic task.

With complete independence, the costs of coordination, C_0, are zero. As greater and greater coordination is achieved, the costs of information processing increases rapidly. The costs of achieving independence, I, have an inverse relationship to the coordination costs. The organization is naturally interested in the sum of these two costs, T_0. The point t_0 represents the ideal compromise between coordination and independence.

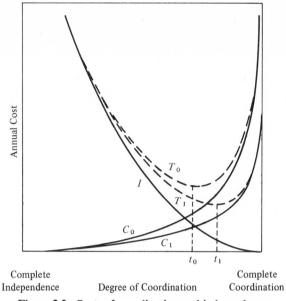

Figure 2-2. Costs of coordination and independence

If improved information technology reduces the cost of providing a given degree of coordination, the coordination-cost curve will shift downward to C_1 and the total-cost curve will move to T_1. As a result, the optimum point shifts to the right to point t_1, where greater coordination is achieved at less total cost. Thus, a reduction in the cost of coordination, as in the case of any other factor of production, encourages its greater use.

The Organization as a Nearly Decomposable System

The optimum tradeoff between independence and coordination lies at neither extreme. Rather, the organization is structured and decoupled in a way that partitions it into relatively isolated subsystems. Relatively isolated means in this case that the interactions *among* subsystems are weak compared to the interactions *within* a given subsystem. Such a system is termed *nearly decomposable.*

Simon and Ando (1961) have demonstrated that a certain type of nearly decomposable system (a linear[8] one) behaves in the short run as a collection of independent subsystems. That is, the behavior of each subsystem—and hence, collectively, the total system—depends in the short run on its own subsystem characteristics; the weak interactions with other subsystems have relatively minor effect. The weak interactions that couple

[8] In a linear system, the response of the system to each disturbance is proportional to the strength of the disturbance, and total behavior is the composite of such individual responses.

31

the separate subsystems do, however, have a cumulative effect. With sufficient time they govern the behavior of the total system.

The concept of near decomposability can be extended to hierarchical systems (Simon and Ando, 1961, p. 137). Thus, each of the weakly-coupled subsystems can itself be a nearly decomposable system. Each of these parts may, in turn, constitute a nearly decomposable system, and so on down to the smallest component. Dynamic behavior may, of course, be different at each level in the system: the "long run" normally becomes progressively shorter as one proceeds down the hierarchy. Thus, high-frequency dynamics are associated with lower-level systems, and low-frequency dynamics with higher-level systems (Simon, 1962, p. 477).

Although an organization by no means constitutes a linear system, it exhibits behavior analogous to that described by the Simon–Ando model. In order to make tractable the task of managing it, the organization is fragmented into a hierarchy of relatively isolated segments through suitable structuring and decoupling. The result is a hierarchical, nearly decomposable system.

Each manager in the organizational hierarchy is able, in the short run, to operate his department relatively free of direction by higher-level managers. The direction that does exist is of an aggregate, rather than a detailed, nature. This direction is transmitted in the form of goals, budgets, schedules, and other types of plans.

But short-term independence does not mean lack of central guidance. The purpose of the higher-level direction is to provide information to lower-level units that causes the organization as a whole to steer toward its global objectives. Long-run behavior can thus be governed by aggregate constraints on the behavior of each subunit. These constraints are, of course, subject to periodic revision in response to new information about the environment and changes in higher-level goals; but, within the confines of the existing constraints, a lower-level manager has relatively great independence.

In generating such constraints, a higher-level manager cannot consider their detailed effects. He necessarily views each lower-level unit in rather aggregate terms. In budgeting, for example, a manager might use a simple cost–volume function to describe the behavior of a subunit. Because of the nature of nearly decomposable systems, aggregate approximations can provide a reasonable basis for describing important interactions and for setting the constraints imposed on the subunits.

Let me summarize this discussion. Because of the limited information-handling ability of both humans and information processing equipment, the organization *must* be constituted as a nearly decomposable system. This is achieved by combining closely related activities and decoupling them from hierarchically more distant activities. The "macro-characteristics" of the organization are governed by relatively aggregate plans issued by higher-level managers. Within the constraints imposed by this information, a lower-level manager then pursues his (changing) goals more or less independently.

This scheme has the essential advantage of economizing on coordination. Higher-level managers adjust lower-level constraints without having to know their detailed implications. Lower-level managers are relatively isolated from the rest of the organization, and can therefore carry on their activities without continual redirection and without constant attention to most of the detailed activities of other parts of the organization.

CHAPTER 3

The Technology of Information Systems

3.1 *The Role of the Information System*

The information system within an organization plays a role analogous to that of the nervous system of an animal. Included in the system are components that perform such functions as the sensing, classification, transmission, storage, retrieval, transformation, and display of information. Its primary purpose is to provide information for decision making and coordination.

The information system is superimposed on an underlying organizational structure. Its channels of communication include the hierarchical links of the organization itself, but also include a great many other channels. The information network thus represents a distinct system designed to furnish information to the various decision nodes within the organization.

The overall information system contains both formal and informal channels. Informal channels include the well-known "grapevine," informal lunchtime conversation in the executive dining room, and casual reading of the *Wall Street Journal*. The essential characteristic of a formal channel is that its existence is explicitly recognized and defined as part of the total system. Its description includes a definition of message content, its source and destination, and perhaps such technical characteristics as message frequency, error rates, urgency, and the like. Although formal channels are often manifested in "hard copy" form, this need not be the case; telephone messages, for example, are a legitimate part of a formal system.

The informal system often fills in the information crevices overlooked by the formal system and thus serves the extremely important role of information backstop. This is particularly true in the case of higher-level decision making, where information requirements are very difficult to anticipate. Nevertheless, an informal system is a fickle crutch. It contains too many unreliable and "noisy" channels for the organization to depend on it as an avowed policy. An information source should therefore be formalized whenever possible. There is a clear trend in this direction. For example, various business intelligence systems have been implemented for collecting, analyzing, and disseminating information from such sources as market research studies, routine reports from salesmen, responses from advertisements, and published material.

In the broadest sense, the information system includes all components involved in decision making, coordination, and monitoring—human as well as automatic. Thus defined, it would include a large portion of the total organization. Such a broad definition avoids the essentially arbitrary (and changing) distinction between human and automatic components, but it also obscures some important differences between the two types of information processor. Accordingly, a somewhat narrower definition will be employed.

As used in the remaining discussion, the term *information system* includes all information processing of a *programmed* nature (March and Simon, 1958, pp. 141–150). This definition excludes that which would normally be considered a "higer-level" or "managerial" decision process. It does specifically include, however, programmed activity associated with the preparation of information inputs to nonprogrammed tasks. It also includes "manual" operations, such as the determination of inventory order quantities based on well-defined procedures. Admittedly, the boundary between programmed and nonprogrammed activities is often a hazy one, but it nevertheless provides a useful way to define an information system.

The output from an information system can be (loosely) classified into two categories. One class consists of information displayed to humans for nonprogrammed decision making. The information presented may simply be extracted from some sort of storage medium. However, it is more likely to result from various transformations on extracted data. The transformations may be relatively simple ones, such as a summary of more detailed data. On the other hand, they may be very complex indeed, as in the case of an elaborate forecasting procedure or a large simulation model.

The other class consists of various kinds of operating information. Production schedules, purchase orders, invoices, and paychecks are a few examples. This information serves as an input to various programmed tasks, whether performed by human or machine. Thus, a production schedule followed by a lathe operator and an analogue signal supplied to a valve by a process control computer are equally valid examples of operating information.[1]

Simon (1960, p. 49) has pointed out that organizations are constructed in three layers: an underlying system of physical processes, a layer of programmed decision processes, and the top layer of nonprogrammed decision processes.[2] Decision-making information is used in the top layer. The decisions made at this level are transmitted to the middle layer in the form of plans. Constrained by such information, the middle layer generates operating information that governs the behavior of the physical processes at the bottom layer.

Input data generally flow counter to decision information. The bulk of the data are collected in connection with the routine processing of transactions. Much of the information for higher-level decision making is then obtained as a by-product of the routine processing. For example, forecasts used in making inventory decisions may be obtained from sales transactions.

3.2 *Functions Performed Within the Information System*

Information systems differ widely in their types of input and output, the transformations performed by the various subsystems, and their structure. Nevertheless, a common set of basic functions can be found in all systems. It will be useful to examine these.

Data Collection

The data collection function captures data about events impinging on the organization and its environment. All information processed by the system must, at one time or another, be collected by some means. Thus data collection serves as the sensory organ of the organization.

[1] Although we will be concerned primarily with internal users of information, various external users also place demands on the system (for example, stockholders, government agencies, and so on).

[2] Rome and Rome (1962a, pp. 524–525) divide the organization into only two layers: a "technological" system and a "governing" system. The latter roughly corresponds to the top two layers of Simon's model.

Data originate throughout the organization, but normally certain lower-level activities have responsibility for the bulk of the collection. The accounting department, for example, collects much of the financial data, and the logistics department (or the equivalent function performed under other names) collects most of the data on physical operations, such as production, inventory levels, shipments, receipts of material, and so forth.

Volume of Data Collected.   An organization of even modest size can generate an enormous volume of data. Every recorded event must be described by some sort of coding scheme, as a means of entering the event into the information system. Depending on the efficiency and completeness of the coding, each such event may give rise to a considerable volume of collected data. A retail sales transaction, for example, conceivably could require the recording of the customer's name, an item identification, price, and any special handling instructions—a total of perhaps fifty characters of data. When multiplied by several thousand sales transactions per day, the task of collecting such a volume of data becomes formidable indeed.

Manufacturing operations can create a similar flood of data. A comprehensive, centralized system for production control, for example, might require the recording of data every time a given production lot completes one of its manufacturing operations. Each of these events may be described by such information as part number, operation completed, machine operator, and current time. In a large shop, many hundreds of these events may occur each day.

Obviously, not all events that occur within the organization are recorded. Most events, in fact, are so totally irrelevant or insignificant that they are ignored by the information system. In many cases, data might have considerable potential value, but the cost of collecting them does not justify the effort. Under these circumstances, one must resort to less precise means of planning and control, such as the use of gross movement of merchandise from warehouse to store rather than detailed store-transaction data. Improvements in data collection techniques—the development of automatic sensing devices, for example—now make it economic to collect data that formerly were ignored.

Methods of Data Collection.   Data collection consists of two steps, sensing and recording.[3] The degree of automation with which these are

---

[3] In addition, conversion of the collected data from one form to another, as is done in keypunching data from a handwritten source document, is often associated with the collection function.

performed can vary from completely manual to completely automatic methods.

A human senses information primarily through sight, as in the reading of a meter or observing boxcar serial numbers. The sense of hearing is also employed, as in the case of a sales clerk filling out a sales slip with information supplied orally by the customer. Even the sense of smell, touch, or taste may occasionally be used.

Often data can be sensed economically by machine. In a processing plant, instruments sense analogue information such as temperature, pressure, and flow rates. Digital information is often sensed automatically in obtaining production figures, traffic counts, and the like.

Sensed information must be recorded in some form before it can be used. The recording medium is usually paper or some sort of magnetic or photographic material. If the data are to be processed further on automatic equipment, they must ultimately be recorded in a machine-readable form such as punched cards or magnetic tape. Therefore, one would like to record data originally in machine-readable form in order to avoid a subsequent manual conversion step.[4]

Reducing the Volume of Data Collection. Capturing data is both expensive and subject to a relatively high rate of error. Often it represents one of the most significant cost elements of operating the information system, and it is the most frequent source of recurring errors. Therefore, substantial savings can be achieved by reducing the volume of data collection.

One obvious way of doing this is simply to monitor the environment less closely. By taking fewer "sample points," one may sometimes reduce the volume of data collection without a corresponding decrease in the value of the information obtained. Indeed, for decision-making and control purposes, a small sample often provides virtually the same information as a 100 per cent sample. However, most data for operating purposes (preparing pay checks, for example) cannot be collected on a sample basis. Furthermore, sampling is limited to relatively repetitive activities.

A more fundamental approach is to avoid collecting the same information more than once. It is an oft-cited maxim of systems design that a given item of data should be collected at only one point in the system and then communicated in machine-readable form to other parts of the system that

[4] Machine readability is a function of technology; some relatively disciplined forms of handwriting can currently be read automatically. See *EDP Analyzer,* August 1965.

need it. For example, sales data collected by the order entry subsystem should serve the needs of accounting, inventory control, production scheduling, and sales analyses.

Still another way of reducing the volume of data collection is to predict rather than collect data. Data are collected in order to sense the current state of the environment. But the typical information system already has access to a great deal of prior information. Often it is better to use such information to predict future events than it is to collect new data after the events have occurred.

For example, when the system generates a purchase order, it also has access to considerable information about the eventual receipt of the material ordered. This event must be described in order to identify the purchase order, supplier, quantity, price, and quality status. Many of these data can be predicted in advance as "fixed" information; only the data difficult or impossible to predict (such as quality status) need be collected as "variable" information when the material is actually received.

Data Classification and Indexing

When an event is recorded, it must be described in some way that permits retrieval of desired information. The purpose of data classification is to associate an event with other events with which it has significant similarities. It does this by identifying the event with various attributes that are relevant for decision-making purposes. Each attribute constitutes a dimension of the classification scheme.

Relevance is a matter of degree; it depends on the purpose at hand (Goetz, 1949, pp. 34–35). For example, in ordering raw material for a manufactured part, the type of material from which it is made is the relevant attribute; for scheduling its production, the labor content of the part becomes relevant. A sales transaction may likewise be described by such attributes as item identification, customer, salesman, time period, industry, and geographic location.

Often different attributes are not independent, but instead exhibit a hierarchy. For example, a given refrigerator might have the following hierarchical classification:

Group: consumer products
Division: major appliances
Product line: refrigerator
Type: model XYZ

"Low-level" decisions (for example, scheduling) may require information about specific models. On the other hand, "high-level" decisions (determination of advertising budgets, say) typically require hierarchically aggregated information, since the finer details are beyond the purview of higher-level decision makers.

If the classification scheme does not recognize a given attribute, there is no way information about that dimension can be obtained (short of reclassifying the data). If, for example, sales data are not classified by geographic region, information about the geographic distribution of sales cannot be obtained. In a very real sense, data are only what the classification system describes them to be.

The aim of the classification scheme is to partition events along significant decision dimensions. This obviously implies that an understanding of the decision processes within the organization must underlie the system of classification (Goetz, 1949, pp. 137–139; Miller and Starr, 1960, pp. 123–124). However, it is normally not possible to predict all relevant dimensions at the time the classification scheme is established. To some extent, therefore, classification is based on speculation about future information needs. On the other hand, one must necessarily limit the number of dimensions, since each attribute adds to the volume of data required to describe an event. An additional dimension may also enormously increase storage requirements if the data are retained in disaggregated form in which each data element is homogenous with respect to all of its attributes.

The choice of attributes is not the only problem that the system designer must face in identifying data. He must also choose index terms for naming the attributes and their values. Suppose, for example, that geographical location by state is a relevant attribute of a sales transaction. The index term selected for naming the attribute could be "geographical location," "geo. loc.," "GL," "state," or any number of other alternatives. The value of this attribute is similarly largely arbitrary: Pennsylvania, Penna., and Pa. are all legitimate alternative ways of identifying the state of Pennsylvania. In a manual system the choice of index terms may not be too crucial, since a human is able to treat alternative terms as synonyms. An automatic system can also allow synonyms, but usually only when explicit provision is made for the use of a given term.[5]

The difficulty of classification and indexing depends greatly on the type of data being dealt with. Financial and logistics data tend to offer relatively few problems. Such data usually deal with well-defined events, the structure of the data is often quite simple, terminology may be fairly easy to stan-

---

[5] Danzis (1965) describes a system capable of automatically recognizing certain types of synonym.

dardize, and the problem exists in a relatively disciplined environment.[6]

The real problems occur when one deals with narrative data, such as technical documents, textual reports, and intelligence information about competitors' activities. Material of this sort tends to have a low information density and an exceedingly variable structure. The classification scheme is designed to mitigate these problems.

The index terms describing narrative data represent an abstraction: they attempt to boil down the essence of the data so that one can reasonably infer content from the index terms alone. This offers the obvious advantage of reducing substantially the data that must be scanned to locate desired information. Index terms also provide the less obvious advantage of a more standard terminology and format.

These advantages carry a risk, however. In most information-retrieval systems, the index terms assigned to an item of data provide the only means of gaining access to the document—its only window to the world, as it were. Since the index terms represent only an abstract description of the data, they cannot convey the full contents of the data they purport to identify. There is always some probability, then, that the system will overlook relevant information.

Data Compression

The volume of data normally generated is so enormous that somehow it must be reduced in order not to swamp the organization with trivial information. The purpose of data compression is to reduce the volume of data communicated throughout the organization without reducing too severely their information content. A number of methods exist for doing this.

Filtering Out Insignificant Information.   The vast bulk of the data introduced into a system have relatively little significance. For the most part, they merely confirm earlier predictions made at the time current activities were being planned.[7] Even when the predictions prove to be faulty, new data may not lead to a significant change in plans. Ideally, the information system should filter out insignificant data and pass on only the "exceptions" that call for the modification of current plans (Ackoff, 1967).

---

[6] Systems designers will recognize this as an outrageous oversimplification of the difficulties involved.

[7] This does not (necessarily) mean that the data should not have been collected in the first place, since in general one cannot know in advance that they were insignificant. Chapter 4 explores this issue in greater depth.

At best, this can be done only imperfectly. Identification of all exceptions requires a complete formalization of the planning process in order to know which plans require revision. This cannot normally be done, and so exception-reporting systems are designed to screen out only the relatively clear-cut nonexceptions that fall within allowed tolerances from a standard. The remainder of the data are identified as exceptions; it is then up to the decision maker to apply more subtle filters to isolate the few critical exceptions. When setting control limits for the screening process, the system designer obviously faces the same problem met in quality control —namely, to balance the error of passing on insignificant data against the error of screening out a true exception. As the decision process becomes better understood, it is possible to reduce both errors simultaneously (analogous to dealing with a larger sample size in quality control).

Aggregation of Data.   Another common method of data compression is to aggregate data over unwanted classification dimensions and thus reduce the volume of displayed data.[8] The usefulness of this process rests on the assumption that the eliminated dimensions are irrelevant for the purpose at hand (but not for all purposes, obviously, or the data should not be classified along the irrelevant dimensions). For example, in controlling factory inventory, sales transactions might be aggregated along the dimensions of customer, salesman, industry, and geographic region, leaving the data classified in terms of the remaining dimensions, item and time period.

Suppose that a given type of data are classified along the dimensions $i, j, k, \ldots, m$. Each *primitive data cell* $d_{ijk \ldots m}$ contains the total value of the events falling within a specific multidimensional class (for example, the total sales of a given item within a given time period to a given customer, and so forth).[9] Thus, all events included within a cell are homogeneous with respect to the classification criteria, and therefore are considered identical events as far as the classification scheme is concerned. If dimensions i and j are the only ones relevant for a given type of decision, the data are aggregated along the remaining dimensions $k, \ldots, m$:[10]

$$d_{ij} = \sum_{k, \ldots, m} d_{ijk \ldots m}$$

[8] It should be noted that such aggregation does not imply that the detailed data are lost in the process. The aggregation may be performed on an *ad hoc* basis from detailed data retained in disaggregated form. This issue is discussed on pages 48–49.

[9] Rather than total value, a cell may contain other attributes. For example, it might contain the number of events, their average sales value, or a list of serial numbers that identify individual sales transactions.

[10] If the values recorded in the data cells are incommensurable, they must be con-

Compression of Probabilistic Data.   Much of the data collected by the organization deal with probabilistic variables. Sales and labor efficiencies, for example, may exhibit rather pronounced random variations. The spurious "noise" component of the data is often filtered out before the information is communicated throughout the organization.

Probabilistic variables can be described in various ways that differ considerably in their degree of compression. The greatest compression is achieved when a variable is described by a single parameter. Often the mean of a probability distribution is used for this purpose, but other parameters may also be used. An "optimistic" sales forecast 10 per cent over the mean of past sales might be used, for instance.

Data compression of this sort serves a twofold purpose. First, it reduces the volume of data communicated. Second—and of more fundamental importance—it creates greater consistency throughout the organization. If the complete set of data were communicated, each user of the data would have to draw his own inferences from them. Different users tend to draw different inferences, for otherwise there would be no advantage in communicating the complete data rather than the common inference. Under these circumstances, activities throughout the organization can become seriously conflicting.

The compression of probabilistic variables into a single parameter represents a form of *uncertainty absorption*. "Uncertainty absorption takes place when inferences are drawn from a body of evidence and the inferences, instead of the evidence itself, are then communicated" (March and Simon, 1958, p. 165). The communicated parameter—a sales forecast, say—provides a common basis for planning throughout the organization and thus achieves consistency.

A strong case can be made for consistent action, even if it is based on false inferences. If the organization has a mechanism for attaining consistent behavior, it is likely to be able to respond adequately to errors in predictions. This is not the case if every fragment of the organization follows its own bent—even if many of the units are "correct" in their predictions.

Despite its advantages, the transmission of a single value to represent a probability distribution obviously suppresses information about the distribution. The desirability of such compression depends on the nature of the

---

verted to a common unit of measure by multiplying by a weighting factor w_k associated with one of the dimensions. If, for example, the data cells contain the number of units of various items sold, aggregation by dollar value could be done by multiplying unit sales by the corresponding unit value.

decision processes that use the information. In general, the decision that maximizes expected utility is not the same as the decision that maximizes utility if unbiased mean estimates are substituted for probability distributions[11] (Theil, 1961, pp. 414–424).

In special circumstances, however, an unbiased estimate of the mean serves as a *certainty equivalent,* in the sense that an optimal decision can be reached when only the mean is used in the decision model (Theil, 1964, pp. 54–59). Even in cases where these special circumstances do not hold, many decision processes tend to be relatively insensitive to the substitution of mean estimates for random variables. For example, Muth (1963) shows that job shop scheduling falls into this category.

If a single value is inadequate, additional information about a distribution can be provided in a number of ways. Rarely is it necessary, however, to supply the complete history of individual events; considerable compression is normally possible (Bellman, 1961, p. 45). Often the mean and variance together define a distribution with adequate precision. An estimate of the probable range of a random variable is sometimes employed. The range, along with an estimate of the mode, is becoming quite familiar in several types of planning in which the three estimated values are usually termed "pessimistic," "most likely," and "optimistic."

Data Storage

Data storage serves the role of memory, allowing the organization to take action based on information about an arbitrarily distant past. Because all current behavior has its seeds in the past (albeit, in some cases the very recent past), lack of a memory would paralyze the organization. Furthermore, all learning and adaptation rely on access to information about past actions and their consequences.

Organization of the Data Base.   The data base consists of the sum total of stored information available to the organization (normally in machine-readable form). In order to facilitate retrieval of information, the data base must be structured in a way that shows important relationships among the data elements. In addition, each data element must have a specified format and must be assigned to a specified (but perhaps varying)

---

[11] Consider, for example, the following two alternatives: (1) receive $1 million with certainty, or (2) receive $5.4 million with probability .2 and lose $100,000 with probability .8. Both have an expected value of $1 million, but they offer vastly different utilities for most of us.

physical storage device. All of these are part of the task of organizing the data base.

One of the important ways of establishing logical relationships among elements is through a hierarchical structure of the data base. Designing this structure involves the same sort of issues faced in determining the structure of any system. Normally the data base is fragmented into (perhaps overlapping) subsets called *files,* each of which contains relatively homogeneous information. For example, separate files might contain information about customers, suppliers, inventory items, employees, and stockholders.

A file has its own hierarchical structure. It consists of a set of *records,* each containing a collection of information pertaining to a particular item. The customer file contains a separate record for each customer, the inventory file a separate record for each item of inventory, and so forth. A record, in turn, is further broken down into *fields.* These, too, may have a still more detailed hierarchical structure. For example, the address field within a customer record may have subfields for street, city, and ZIP code.[12]

Not all important relationships can be shown through this hierarchical structure. Raw-material inventory records and supplier records, for instance, are typically stored as part of separate files. Neither type of record "belongs to" or is part of the other, and so they cannot be organized hierarchically. And yet the data base must reveal such relationships as the suppliers of a given material or the materials sold by a given supplier. In many cases multiple relationships exist between a record and other records —a raw material, say, may be a component of several parts, it may currently have an outstanding purchase requisition, and it may have other materials that can serve as substitutes. Relationships such as these are established through various forms of cross-references that link one record with others.

Identification of Stored Data.   Stored data[13] must obviously be identified in some way. The identification can be either explicit or implicit. If data are identified explicitly, an appropriately coded label or tag is attached

---

[12] Any good basic text on data processing, such as Gregory and Van Horn (1963), describes file organization in much more detail than is appropriate here. More recent developments are discussed in *EDP Analyzer,* February 1966, November 1966, and December 1967.

[13] Some authors differentiate between *information* and *data,* using *information* to mean data processed into some meaningful form. But the usefulness of information is a matter of degree. Furthermore, in a hierarchical structure one man's information is another man's data. From an operational standpoint, the distinction is difficult to make.

to the data. Each record, for example, normally includes an identification field called its *key*. Less commonly, a field within a record may have an associated identification tag—labeling it as the address field within a customer record, for example.

Often the identification of data is not stated explicitly, but is instead implicit in the position of the data—either absolute physical position or the position relative to other data. A customer's address, for example, might always be stored in the third field of the customer record.

Both schemes offer advantages and disadvantages. The great advantage of implicit identification is that it eliminates the need for storing a label along with the substantive data. Processing procedures are simplified and speeded by the standard format of stored data. On the other hand, in cases where data are highly variable, forcing them into a standard format may be very wasteful of storage space. If, for example, not all employees have had university training, it may be wasteful to reserve a portion of every employee record for a description of university education. Furthermore, the algorithm for processing implicitly identified data must itself contain information about the standard data format, since the data are in no way self-defining.

Explicit identification eliminates the disadvantages of implicit identification, but at the cost of introducing some of its own. Explicit labels contain information and hence increase the storage requirements for each data field so identified. However, only the relevant fields require this labeling; empty fields are omitted altogether. If the proportion of empty fields is sufficiently large, explicit identification reduces storage requirements.[14] As the classification scheme becomes "finer," the fraction of empty fields tends to increase and explicit identification becomes relatively more economical of storage space.

Storage Media.   Any medium that can assume two or more stable states can be used for storing data. The data are coded in such a way that a one-to-one correspondence exists between a given data value and a pattern of stable states. For data that are to be processed by machine, there are obvious advantages in storing information in a form that can be read directly by some automatic sensing device.

Magnetic media offer unique combinations of properties that make them the most widely used form of storage. Besides the advantage of being

---

[14] If s is the average size of substantive data fields (in characters, say), c the average size of an explicit identification code, and f the fraction of empty fields, then explicit identification requires less storage space if $(s + c)(1 - f) < s$.

machine readable, magnetic devices offer a wide range of volumes, cost, and access times (that is, the time required to obtain information once it has been called for). As one might expect, tradeoffs exist between these characteristics. For example, the fastest storage devices, with access times of considerably less than one microsecond (that is, one millionth of a second) have a cost of perhaps seven orders of magnitude greater than the cost of bulk storage using off-line[15] magnetic tape.

Storage Hierarchy.   Because of the vast differences in volume, speed, and cost, the data base is typically stored in a hierarchy of physical storage devices (not necessarily corresponding to its *logical* structure). Table 3-1 gives order-of-magnitude estimates for performance characteristics of various storage devices. A system may employ devices from several (or all) of the levels shown.

Table 3-1. Physical Storage Hierarchy

Level of Storage and Examples of Devices	Representative Order-of-Magnitude Characteristics		
	Volume (Bits*)	Access Time (μsec)	Cost ($/Bit)
1. Ultra high speed: diodes, read-only storage	$10^3 - 10^4$	$<10^{-1}$	$10^0 - 10^1$
2. High speed immediate access: magnetic core, thin film	$10^6 - 10^7$	10^0	10^{-1}
3. Bulk immediate access: magnetic core	10^8	10^1	$>10^{-2}$
4. On-line direct access: magnetic drum, disk, cartridge	$10^8 - 10^{10}$	$10^4 - 10^6$	$<10^{-4} - <10^{-2}$
5. Off-line: magnetic tape, removable disk or cartridge	$>10^{11}$	10^8	$10^{-7} - <10^{-5}$

* The capacity of a storage device can be expressed in bits (for *binary digit*), which (roughly) is the amount of information that can be represented by a two-state device. It normally requires six to eight bits to represent a given alphabetic character, decimal digit, or special symbol (for example, $, +, or −).

A given item of data must be allocated to one of the devices comprising the storage hierarchy. In order to minimize average access time, data having the highest probability of retrieval should be allocated to the storage devices

[15] *On-line* storage is storage that is accessible to a computer without the need for human intervention, whereas *off-line* storage requires such intervention (for example, mounting a magnetic tape reel on the read–write unit).

having the shortest access time.[16] Since these probabilities tend to vary greatly over time, depending on the age of data and the processing sequence followed, data may be continually shifted from one level to another in order to maintain an efficient allocation. Although certain "overhead" costs are associated with the transfer of data between levels and maintaining a directory of their current location, dynamic allocation of data can vastly increase the performance of the system.

The probability of referring to a piece of data tends to decline with its age. When a recorded event occurs, data describing it are stored in the data base. After a relatively short time the data may cease to have much individual value for low-level planning. They are then aggregated with other data for use in higher-level planning. This same process may be repeated several times, and with each repetition the data become more aggregated and are preserved over a longer period of time (corresponding to the longer cycles of higher-level planning). In the meantime, the detailed data may be transferred to a lower level in the storage hierarchy. Eventually these data may be discarded altogether or stored on some very low cost but relatively inaccessible medium (microfilm, say) in order to provide emergency backup and to meet various archival requirements.

The point at which data should be discarded or assigned to a lower level in the storage hierarchy is very much a function of cost. This cost includes not only the cost of storage, but also the cost of retrieving desired data. As these costs go down—as they decidedly have done during the past two decades—the organization should preserve detailed data in accessible form for a longer period of time.

Keeping data in disaggregated form certainly magnifies the costs of storage and retrieval. However, the alternative seems even less palatable. If the organization insists on discarding detailed data (or storing them in an inaccessible medium), the system designer is then forced to select which of the possible alternative aggregations will be preserved. The number of alternatives is so vast, and information needs are so difficult to anticipate,

---

[16] To be more precise, the allocation of storage should be such that the expected value of stored information is maximized. Expected value equals the probability of retrieval times the value of the information for a given response time. If the value drops sharply with increased response time, the information should be allocated to a storage medium with a short access time. In practice, it is difficult to estimate the relationship between value and response time, and so only the probability of retrieval is usually used (as estimated from the time interval since the last reference). In most systems it is possible for the user to define maximum and minimum levels in the hierarchy for a given item of data in order to keep the response time within suitable limits.

that useful information inevitably gets washed out by the aggregation process. This is one of the reasons why conventional systems so frequently cannot meet the information requirements of the organization (*EDP Analyzer,* April 1967).

The ability to store primitive data and aggregate them on an *ad hoc* basis offers the only real solution to this problem. To be sure, the technical requirements for such a system are quite demanding, but they are by no means beyond present capabilities. It is becoming increasingly feasible to store, retrieve, and manipulate vast quantities of detailed data. These advances strongly militate in favor of maintaining a much more detailed data base than formerly was feasible.[17]

Data Management

The objective of the data management function is to provide access to information contained in the data base. It serves as the interface between the storage hierarchy and the various information processes that use or modify the contents of the data base. This includes human decision making and such application programs as payroll calculations and inventory control.

Requirements of Data Management.   Data management is one of the most critical aspects of the entire information system. In order for the system to serve the needs of the organization, the data management function should meet the following requirements.

Efficient routine processing.   The bulk of the information retrieved from the data base is used in the preparation of routine, periodic reports and operating documents. Consequently, considerable attention should be paid to the efficiency of the system in processing these outputs.

One of the ways of increasing efficiency is to segment the data base into separate files such that a given type of processing requires access to relatively homogeneous data records. For example, inventory records are typically maintained in a separate file. Each record contains all of the data necessary to update inventory balances and to perform inventory control calculations. With such organization, the inventory program need only access a limited and well-defined segment of the data base. Furthermore, the records are usually maintained in a standard sequence, such as by item

---

[17] As a matter of efficiency, it may be advantageous to store frequently used summary data in their aggregate form (in addition to the detailed data). In this way, one avoids repeated aggregation of the same detailed data.

identification number, and all new transactions describing recent events (an inventory withdrawal, say) are batch processed in the same sequence. This permits the processing of all transactions with only one pass over the complete inventory file.

Data management for batch processing of this sort is relatively simple. The organization of each record and the identification of each data element are known perfectly by the person writing the program. Therefore, it is feasible to incorporate the data management function as an integral part of each routine program. The task is made easier for the programmer by the use of standard programmed software[18] that handles some of the messy details of controlling the transfer of data between the processor and the storage hierarchy.

Ad hoc inquiries. For reasons discussed earlier, systems designers cannot predict in advance and prepare on a periodic basis all of the information that will be needed within the organization. Future information requirements are not merely unknown, they are unknowable. The data management function should therefore be able to provide information that could not be anticipated in detail. Such information is provided by the system in response to *ad hoc* inquiries.[19]

Ideally, a response provides all of the information, and only the information, needed to satisfy a given inquiry. This is not an unreasonable goal when the data being retrieved have a well-defined structure. For example, a manager might want to know the total dollar sales of product X in region Y. He would expect a single dollar value as a response to a suitably framed inquiry. Similarly, a well-defined response can be given to an inquiry calling for a list of all engineers within the organization having specified professional qualifications.

---

[18] Actual physical equipment constitutes the *hardware* of a computer system. The collection of general computer programs available to the user constitutes the computer's *software*. These include language translators, operating systems that manage computer resources, and utility packages such as sort programs (Hammer, 1967). The decision to perform a given task through hardware or through software is a technical–economic question. Current developments in electronics (for example, large-scale integrated circuits) move the tradeoff point toward greater reliance on hardware.

[19] This does not imply that conventional periodic reports do not serve a useful purpose. If information has a sufficiently high probability of being retrieved, it is usually less expensive to supply it on a routine basis than on an *ad hoc* basis. The telephone company, for example, finds it advantageous to supply its subscribers with a complete listing of all telephone numbers, even though the vast majority of the numbers are of absolutely no value to any given subscriber. The alternative to this would be to provide enough information operators to respond to all requests for specific numbers. See *EDP Analyzer,* June 1965 and January 1967.

The required response to an inquiry often does not exist as such in storage, particularly if data are stored in detailed form. However, it may still be logically possible to compute a suitable response as a function of the data base. For example, suppose monthly unit sales data are stored only by county for each item in a company's product line. In this case, a correct response to the inquiry, "What were total dollar sales in Pennsylvania in 1964?", cannot be obtained merely through extracting a field of stored data. Instead, the response must be computed by aggregating more primitive data.

Computation is also involved in inquiries that call for counting, finding maximum or minimum values, or determining the value of common statistical parameters such as the standard deviation. In some cases the required computation may be very complex indeed. "What if . . ." questions are often of this type. For example, a response to the inquiry, "What would happen to the return-on-investment figure if sales decline 10 per cent?", may involve an elaborate simulation in order to calculate the predicted consequences of the change.[20]

Information retrieval involving some form of computation is clearly a more complex problem than mere extraction. The user of the system, however, need not be made aware that his inquiry involves computation. To the extent possible, the program to retrieve primitive data and transform them in the desired way should be generated automatically as an implication of the actual (high-level) inquiry.[21] Obviously, if the computation required is not of a fairly standard type, the person framing the inquiry must spell out in more or less detail (depending on the particular system) the procedures required for manipulating extracted data.

The retrieval of data can be viewed as the inverse operation to the original classification process. Thus, if T is the transformation used in classification and T^{-1} is the inverse transformation, then

$$T(\text{data stored}) = \text{index terms}$$
$$\text{and } T^{-1}(\text{index terms}) = \text{data retrieved}$$

The person submitting an inquiry tries to formulate it so that he will receive relevant data in response. His success in this depends on his ability

[20] A problem of terminology arises here. Defined broadly enough, information retrieval includes *all* information processing. Some authors consider information retrieval to involve only the extraction of data. However, several retrieval systems include facilities for obtaining counts, aggregations, and common statistical parameters. It seems worthwhile to include at least this computation capability within the scope of information retrieval.

[21] See, for example, a discussion of the "Baseball" system by Green *et al.* (1961).

to judge how the relevant data are indexed—that is, he tries to estimate the transformation T. He then attempts to frame his inquiry such that

$$T^{-1}(\text{inquiry}) = \text{relevant data}$$

The inquiry must, of course, be expressed in some sort of language. This is true whether the request for information is given to a clerk or to a computer. A clerk, however, is usually more tolerant of ambiguities than are automatic retrieval languages. If the clerk cannot interpret an ambiguous inquiry, he can often dispel most ambiguities through a probing dialogue with the inquirer.

Whether or not it is done so explicitly, an unambiguous inquiry must be expressed in a form equivalent to a logical, or Boolean, expression. Such an expression may be formed from the Boolean operators *not, and, or,* and from the *relational operators* $<$, $\leq$, $=$, $\geq$, $>$, $\neq$. The *operands* on which they operate may be various index terms or (in the case of the relational operators) numbers or arithmetic expressions.[22]

If one wants to do more than merely extract stored data, the language must provide a means of specifying the algorithm to be used in manipulating extracted data. Conceivably this could vary all the way from a general algorithmic language (such as Algol or Fortran) to a very limited set of operations. As an example of the latter approach, a retrieval language might include such "verbs" as *list, count,* and *sum.*

The following examples of inquiries illustrate the use of a hypothetical retrieval language providing the capabilities discussed:[23]

1. List products with sales in Massachusetts > 1000.
2. Count salesmen with sales > 1000000 and years-service < 10.
3. Sum products with inventory $> 1.3 \times$ (Order-point + order-quantity) and inventory $\times$ unit-price > 5000.

These illustrations by no means exhaust the logical possibilities provided by a general retrieval language. For example, an inquirer might wish to search with "relaxed" conditions, calling for only a partial satisfaction

---

[22] The specific form of Boolean expressions may vary from one language to another. A well-defined form is that of Algol (*algo*rithmic *l*anguage) described by Naur (1963, p. 8).

[23] The examples are purely for illustration, and are not taken from any specific language. An actual retrieval language must include a number of other features, such as the ability to specify output content and format, to rearrange the sequence of data, and so forth. A description of such a language is contained in Postley (1968).

of multiple search criteria (Ledley, 1962, pp. 506–510). In other cases, one might want to assign varying weights to different search criteria, retrieving an item if its total weight exceeds a specified threshold value.

Expanded capabilities of this kind increase the complexity of specifying desired data. However, the complexity stems not from the retrieval language, but from the logical complexity of specifying precisely what information is wanted out of a very large data base. As the size, variety, and complexity of the data base grow, increased information must be provided in some form in order to select the relatively very small set of data required to satisfy a given inquiry. This selection information is, of course, supplied by the inquiry itself. The aim of the retrieval language is to facilitate the logical specification of the selection information.

As difficult as it may sometimes be, the logical specification of desired data does not end the problem of retrieving the data. In most cases, the inquiry only specifies *what* data are wanted; it does not specify *how* they are to be retrieved. Somehow the inquiry must be translated from *declarative* form (the "what" specification) into *procedural* form (the "how" specification). If the translator does its work faithfully, the two specifications are logically equivalent.

In an automatic system using computers for the actual retrieval, the search algorithm must ultimately be expressed in the form of a very detailed procedural specification written in the machine code of the computer. In order to make *ad hoc* inquiries feasible, the computer itself must perform the translation.[24] Several such systems already exist, but unfortunately they are not widely used in the routine business of managing an organization.

In formulating an inquiry, one must specify the index terms corresponding to the desired data. The identification of data presents no problem if the inquirer has complete knowledge of the classification scheme. For example, sales data might be classified according to a perfectly standard and well-defined system. An inquirer seeking such data would find no difficulty in correctly identifying the data he seeks—the dollar sales of product X in Pennsylvania, say.

This relatively straightforward case does not always exist, however. Various degrees of uncertainty may surround the classification system. The inquirer wanting sales data, for example, may not know the precise

---

[24] I am dismissing rather cavalierly a number of difficult practical problems that must be faced in performing the translation. For example, the organization of the data base—the physical location of various records and the means of locating them— has a vital bearing on the choice of a detailed search algorithm.

terminology used in identifying the state of Pennsylvania. Should he identify it by spelling out the name in full, by an abbreviation, or perhaps by some numeric code?

Often problems of this sort can be eliminated during the process of translating the inquiry into the procedural search algorithm. An intelligent clerk, for instance, could easily handle inquiries in which the state is variously identified as "Pennsylvania," "Pa.," "Penn.," "Penna.," or even "Pensilvania." Considerable tolerance for variation and errors in identification can also be built into an automatic retrieval system, although often at a rather high cost.

This example only hints at some of the difficulties encountered when the inquirer has less than complete knowledge about the classification scheme. He may even be largely ignorant of the contents of the data base. Document retrieval often represents the extreme case in which the inquirer has relatively little information about either the classification scheme or the contents of the document library. In trying to retrieve documents about a given subject, the inquirer is often attempting to communicate with an unknown person (the classifier of the desired documents) using abstract terminology describing an unknown set of documents.

Suppose, for example, that the inquirer were looking for information about "information systems," and suppose further (just for the sake of illustration) that he would consider this book a relevant response. The classifier might appropriately use any number of classification terms, such as "systems," "information systems," "data processing," "computers," "planning and control," and "organization theory." Each term, or any set of them, gives a far from complete characterization. The abstract nature of the indexing would be largely immaterial if the classifier could accurately predict the index terms used by inquirers (or vice versa), but this is often not the case.

All of the numerous difficulties mentioned render the general data retrieval problem essentially "unsolvable." This is so because neither the contents of the data base nor the inquirer's desired information can, in general, be described precisely, but only in very abstract terms. Whenever the abstraction used in describing the data base by means of index terms does not correspond to the description contained in inquiries, various errors in retrieval will occur.

Because of the inherent difficulty of the problem, it is doubtful that any information retrieval system can be successful unless it allows the user to zero in gradually, in hierarchical fashion, on the information he desires (as in the game of Twenty Questions, but without the constraint that questions can have only a yes–no response.) This is the essential characteristic of the skilled librarian: by repeated probes the librarian can localize the area of search to a small part of the total data base. An automatic system should offer comparable facilities. In effect, the user should be able to engage in a dialogue with the system so that the two can come to a mutual understanding about the desired information. (This scheme is probably feasible only if the user has on-line access to the system in order to gain relatively short response times.)

Some relatively primitive versions of such a system have already been implemented (Rome and Rome, 1962b; Summers and Bennett, 1967). They typically employ a hierarchical classification scheme for all stored data. At each level in the hierarchy the person making an inquiry is presented with a display of the available classifications. When a choice is made (as signaled through a keyboard, say), the computer displays the next level down the selected path of the hierarchy. One can thus penetrate very quickly to a detailed description of any data included in the system.

Not all information can be classified conveniently in a neat hierarchical fashion, but the concept of an ever-narrowing search is a very powerful one, nevertheless. A hierarchical classification system automatically defines similarity by proximity in the tree structure. In the absence of such a classification scheme, similarity must be established through such means as term associations having varying weights.

The process of data retrieval can now be summarized as follows. There exists a set of stored formal data called the data base. For any given inquiry there exists a "relevant" subset of these data (possibly an empty set); all remaining data form an "irrelevant" subset.[25] The inquirer attempts to describe the relevant set in terms of an inquiry. This is then matched with a description of the entire set of data described in terms of a classification scheme. As a result of this matching, certain data are retrieved and all other data are rejected. Thus, the total data base is partitioned into four subsets:

1. Relevant and retrieved.
2. Irrelevant and rejected.
3. Relevant and rejected.
4. Irrelevant and retrieved.

The object in designing a retrieval system is obviously to make the latter two subsets as small as possible (for a given expenditure of resources). Only in special cases are both subsets empty; in general, one must strike a

[25] Since relevance is normally a matter of degree, "relevant" data can be thought of as having a relevance that exceeds some threshold level.

balance between retrieving too much irrelevant data and too little relevant data.[26]

Security. The data base represents a resource of almost incalculable value to the organization, and so its integrity must be closely protected. Serving as the interface between the data base and various uses of information, the data management function has responsibility for maintaining security of the data base. Three different aspects of security must be considered: backup protection against loss or destruction, validity, and privacy.

Backup protection is provided through duplication. In most systems the information stored on each physical storage file (for example, a reel of magnetic tape or a disk file) is duplicated in some form. Often the backup is stored at a lower level in the storage hierarchy—when, for example, a disk is used as backup for a drum or when tape is used as backup for a disk.

In the case of magnetic tape, in which updating of the file requires preparation of a new physical reel of tape (since the contents of the old reel cannot be changed selectively), backup is provided as an inherent by-product of processing. (Steps must still be taken, of course, to preserve until the next updating cycle the old reel and the transactions processed against it.) When portions of the data base are changed selectively instead of through copying (as in most systems employing magnetic drum or disk), special provision must be made to provide backup. The usual approach is to record periodically on a backup file the current contents of the file being protected.

In order to keep the data base a faithful image of reality, the data-management function must maintain the validity of data entering the system. Typically, the data base already contains considerable prior information about entering data—their format, allowed character mode (for example, alphabetic or numeric), and the set or range of permitted values. The entering data are thus partially redundant. This provides a means to test for validity. If the entering data meet all checks as to format, range, and so forth, they are assumed to be valid.

Redundancy obviously cannot be sufficient to guarantee complete validity, because this would require prior information about correct data values and consequently no new information would be received. Nevertheless, validity checks can screen out many common errors and can usually call into question a "large" error that might otherwise create havoc if

---

[26] The probability of making these two types of error is analogous to the "consumer's risk" (acceptance of defective items) and "producer's risk" (rejection of acceptable items) in statistical quality control.

allowed to enter the system. A "small" error is much more difficult to identify, but failure to detect it often results in relatively minor consequences.

The data management function should provide easy, but not indiscriminate, access to the data base. Certain portions may be completely private to a specified class of user, and therefore should be protected against all intrusions by unauthorized persons. The contents of other segments may be examined, but not altered, by prescribed users. Still other segments may be made completely accessible. The data management function should therefore be designed to allow partitioning of the data base into segments having selective accessibility for examining or changing data elements.

Generality and flexibility. The data management function should be able to accommodate changes in requested output. This ability can be provided in part through a generalized system capable of responding to *ad hoc* inquiries. In order to deal with changes not included within the scope of an existing inquiry language, the system should also be able to accept new algorithms or procedures for operating on data extracted from the data base.

In some cases it may be impossible to provide requested information, no matter how general or flexible the system is in transforming stored data. The desired information may simply not be a function of the current data base. In order to handle these situations, the data base should be able to accept new data and to restructure or delete existing data. This is difficult to do if the logical organization of the data base (that is, the relationships among the data elements) is tied too closely to its physical organization (that is, the allocation of data elements among physical storage devices). It is possible to achieve partial separation between logical and physical organization by identifying each data element by a symbolic name and maintaining a directory that associates a symbolic name with the current physical location of the corresponding data element.

Data Management Systems.   A data management function that meets the requirements for routine processing, security, generality, and flexibility has to be enormously complex. The complexity is great enough that we cannot afford the luxury of developing a complete specialized function for each application. Specialized systems therefore necessarily slight some requirements. Because of the historical pattern set by the limited capacity of earlier data processing equipment, as well as fairly strong institutional biases in measuring systems performance, most specialized data management functions concentrate heavily on the efficiency of processing routine transactions. They suffer particularly heavily in meeting the requirements for generality and flexibility.

Current technology does not demand so narrow a view of the data management function. The cost of storage and processing has fallen enough that efficiency need not be the overriding consideration that it once was. Advanced systems are now available that meet the other requirements much more fully than most present systems. We have a critical need for generalized systems that handle the data management function for a variety of applications. A few such systems have already been implemented, and a great effort is currently going on to extend present capabilities.[27]

Computation

The computation function consists of all processes within the information system that transform input data into output data. Included among these transformations are the obvious ones associated with the many numeric calculations that are performed in the typical system—calculation of payrolls and invoices, preparation of accounting data, and the like. Many systems also include numerous "optimizing" programs and other forms of decision-making algorithm. These sometimes call for an exceedingly elaborate series of calculations, as in the determination of the "optimum" operating conditions for a petroleum refinery using a linear programming model. Through the development of models of various activities within the organization, planning and control are becoming increasingly computational in nature.

The computation function also includes data manipulation of a non-numeric nature. The ordering of a large number of records according to their identifier (or key) is an example of such an operation. Simulation models often require very complex manipulation of both numeric and nonnumeric data. A search through the data base in order to retrieve and aggregate desired information also involves computation. In short, any well-defined symbol manipulation, whether or not the symbols stand for numeric quantities, represents a form of computation.

The bulk of the data manipulated come from the data base. The data base goes through a continual process of rearrangement, modification,

[27] For a good discussion of some current data management systems, see the following issues of *EDP Analyzer:* May 1965, October 1965, December 1966, December 1967, and January 1968. Minker and Sable (1967) provide an excellent survey of the field and an extensive bibliography.

additions, and deletions in order to keep it a current image of the organization. All of these changes are effected through some sort of computation.

Data used to modify the contents of the data base enter the information system in the form of *transactions*. A transaction represents a coded description of an external event, such as a sale, the completion of a manufacturing operation, or a change in the price of a raw material. Transactions are processed against the data base in order to maintain it as a current image of the organization and its environment. This entails the matching of each transaction with corresponding data base records. For example, a sales transaction must be matched against the record for the customer placing the order and against the record for each item included in the sales order.

Processing may take place in either *sequential* or *random* fashion. Sequential processing means that transactions are handled in the order in which the corresponding records are physically located in the data base. Suppose, for example, that inventory records are maintained in a separate inventory file in part number sequence. Sequential processing of inventory transactions therefore takes place in part number sequence. Random processing means that transactions are processed in an order independent of the physical position of the corresponding data base records. Processing may take place, for example, in event sequence. One type of transaction (for example, an inventory withdrawal) may immediately follow an entirely different type of transaction (for example, an inquiry into a personnel record).

In no other field of technology have recent advances been as great as in computation. Computation speed has been increased by a factor of at least a million in the past two decades. Neither atomic energy nor aerospace technology has ushered in comparable increases in its respective area. Such a fantastic increase in speed, along with the concomitant reduction in the cost of computation, simply cannot be absorbed within our society over such a short period of time. We are only now beginning to perceive some of the effects on the organization brought about by the availability of such a superabundance of computation capacity.

Data Transmission

Data transmission involves communication between geographically separated points. The communication of information can be effected by physical movement of the medium on which the data are recorded—paper or magnetic tape, for example—or by transmission of an electrical signal in which the information is coded. Both methods are employed even in the most modern systems, but electrical transmission is assuming increasing importance.

Data transmission can often be justified on the grounds that centralized computation provides substantial economies compared to the same computation performed on a dispersed or decentralized basis. For one thing, centralized computation requires less total capacity, since it tends to smooth out the load coming from various parts of the organization. If each subunit has to provide for its own computational needs, it must ensure that sufficient capacity is available to meet its peak load. In most cases considerable variation exists in the capacity required over the normal cycle of activity, and therefore matching capacity to the peak requirements usually results in some excess capacity during most of the cycle.[28] Unless the individual peak periods in all subunits happen to coincide, the peak aggregate load will be less than the sum of the separate peaks.

Centralization in computation not only reduces the total capacity required; it also reduces the cost per unit of computation by exploiting economies of scale. According to "Grosch's Law," the cost of a computer system using a given state of the art varies roughly with the square root of computer capacity.[29] Assuming this approximation to be valid, consider the economies of scale in an organization with four subunits, each requiring about the same computational capacity. If the cost per computer suitable for the separate subunits is D, then the total cost is $4D$. The computer cost with centralized computation would only be $\sqrt{4}D = 2D$, or only one-half as much as the decentralized system.

Centralization of computing also permits the use of a computer with a relatively large primary memory. This expands the software available for the system. It also often makes it considerably easier to handle complex tasks by allowing the programmer to avoid some of the difficulties associated with stringent conservation of memory.

The figure just cited considers only the cost of computation; to it must be added the cost of transmitting data between the separate subunits and the centralized computer. This cost depends primarily on distance and the volume of data transmitted (or, more precisely, the channel capacity of the transmission link). Message urgency and the variation in message load also affect cost, since they govern the extent to which channel capacity

---

[28] There are obvious economies in shifting parts of the peak load to off-peak periods. However, response-time requirements often will not permit this.

[29] Knight (1966 and 1968) discusses this issue in some detail.

can be reduced by delaying some (less urgent) messages until offpeak periods. Still other factors, such as reliability and accuracy requirements, may influence the cost of data transmission.

Also offsetting the advantages of a large central computer is the added overhead cost of serving a wide variety of decentralized applications. Some applications may have specialized computing requirements that can be met more cheaply and reliably by a local, specialized computer. Perhaps the ideal arrangement is a network with a large central computer and several small decentralized computers. The small computers can provide modest capacity at quite low cost (Mathews, 1968). They can be used to serve specialized needs, handle "small" local jobs, and perform some compression of data transmitted to the central computer. The central computer would be reserved for "large" jobs and those tasks that inherently require access to a central data base.

In many cases the most important justification for data transmission is that it permits planning on a more global basis. Organizational subunits are often separated geographically, but their activities may nevertheless be highly interacting. For example, one plant might furnish intermediate chemicals to a distant plant, or a group of dispersed warehouses might be supplied out of a common manufacturing facility.

In these circumstances, rapid communications is a prerequisite for close coordination. Lacking such communications, geographically separated subunits would have to resort to increased buffer inventories and slack resources in order to gain greater independence. Close coordination, on the other hand, permits closer coupling of the subunits, with a resulting reduction in the cost of maintaining extra inventory and other resources.

In some cases more rapid data transmission (and data processing) can be traded for slower, and more economical, physical distribution. For example, a centralized sales order processing system that is linked to regional sales offices might permit delivery out of a consolidated warehouse. Without rapid order processing, it may be necessary to maintain a number of regional warehouses in order to make deliveries within a suitable overall lead time.

Technical developments in data transmission have been almost as dramatic as those in computation.[30] It is becoming increasingly feasible to link widely separated activities in order to take advantage of the economies

---

[30] On the basis of current tariffs, data-transmission exhibits about the same cost–volume relationship as computation—namely, costs are roughly proportional to the square root of channel capacity.

of centralized computation and closer coordination. Continuing technological progress provides great impetus for providing a more global data
base for decision making within the organization.

Data Display

The display function is concerned with the preparation of output information in a form for human perception. It thus provides the communications
interface between the information system and members of the organization. Human decisions that govern the behavior of the organization are
based on information displayed in one form or another, and so the effectiveness of this interface plays an important role in the success of the organization.

Not all output data are displayed. Much of the information stays within
the system and merely modifies the data base (and subsequently all processes that use the modified part of the data base). Other output data may
be used to control the environment directly, as in a closed-loop process
control system.

The vast bulk of displayed information is sensed visually. Such information is coded by means of lines and symbols having different shape, size,
color, width, length, intensity, and so forth. Conventional visual displays
have either a narrative or tabular format, in which information is coded
in the form of a relatively limited set of symbols (such as the alphabetic
characters and decimal digits). These displays are primarily prepared by
printers that convert stored data into "hard copy" form.

Graphical display is becoming increasingly attractive. In cases where
high precision is not required—which is certainly true of most decision
making—a graph can often display complex relationships in a far more
compact and comprehensible form than an equivalent tabular report (Sisson, 1960, pp. 105–106 and 112–113). The high cost of preparing graphs
manually has heretofore limited their use, but various display devices are
now available that make it feasible to generate graphical displays cheaply
and rapidly. These displays may be in either a temporary form, as in a
cathode ray tube (CRT), or in regular hard copy form.[31]

Display need not be limited to visual sensing. For example, some recent
automatic information systems employ a very common audio display device,
the telephone. The great advantage of this device is its widespread availability and low cost. Audio (and sometimes tactile) displays are also

---

[31] For some purposes the common printer can be used to prepare adequate, low-
resolution graphical displays. See, for example, Forrester, 1961, pp. 379–381.

used when additional information would saturate the visual sensory chan- nels—as when an alarm is sounded when a pilot fails to lower his landing gear during landing. However, because of the relatively low channel capac- ity of the nonvisual senses, these devices are limited to displaying small volumes of information.

The display function plays a particularly vital role in *man–machine* information systems (see Section 5.8). Such a system has as an essential characteristic the sharing of a common task between a man and a com- puter. If this "symbiosis" is to be a fruitful one, a very close rapport must exist between the man and the machine (Licklider, 1960).

Gaining such rapport is essentially a matter of efficient communications —from the man to the computer and from the computer to the man (Taylor, 1967). This two-way communication has been achieved most successfully so far through the use of CRT display consoles. By means of a movable pointer of some sort (for example, a "light pen" or a cross hair), one can draw on the face of the display tube or point to specific portions of displayed data. Supplemental information can be entered by means of a keyboard or other standard input devices. In this way the man can maintain close direction over the activities of the computer, and the responses from the computer can be displayed immediately to the man.[32]

3.3 *Integrated Information Systems*

An "integrated" or "total" information system seems to be a common goal for all designers of information systems. If these terms have any mean- ing at all, they suggest a more tightly coupled system with less independence among its parts. There are two aspects to such integration: (1) closer coupling of the information system itself, and (2) an information system that allows closer coupling of the various parts of the organization. These are obviously related, but each deserves separate discussion.

Closer Coupling of the Information System

An information system, like all systems, can be designed with different degrees of independence among its parts. Historically, information sub- systems have required considerable independence simply because the infor- mation-processing capacity at the disposal of the designers was so limited

[32] Martin (1967, pp. 76–121 and 295–313) discusses display hardware and its applications.

that the job could be handled only on a highly fragmented basis. This fragmentation is manifested primarily in data collection, file organization, and the scope of computation.

In a fragmented information system, each subsystem is responsible for collecting its own data. Coordination of data collection among multiple subunits within the organization requires relatively advanced means of providing access to shared portions of the data base. With only limited information–handling capability, it is often cheaper to duplicate data collection than it is to perform the coordination necessary to avoid it.

For a given set of operations performed within an information system, a certain number of accesses must be made to the data base in the process of storing and retrieving data. If the state of information technology severely limits the rate of transfer of information to and from a storage medium, the designer has no choice but to fragment the data base into a number of separate files. Furthermore, each file must be largely self-contained with respect to the processing performed on its stored data, for otherwise the coordination required to handle the flow of information among a network of files soon gets out of hand. Since the processes performed on the separate files inevitably require a great deal of common data, a high degree of fragmentation of the data base always implies some duplication of stored data. Duplication, in turn, increases the cost of storage, creates difficult problems of reconciling different files that purport to contain common data, and makes consistency throughout the organization all but impossible.[33]

Limited capacity for storing, retrieving, and manipulating data forces a fragmentation of the processes that operate on each of the separate files. Thus, one process might be used to "maintain" a file (add, delete, or modify records within the file), and another to extract desired information. Each process requires access to the file, and therefore fragmented processing entails duplicate retrieval of data. As a result, processing costs are increased and the effective accessibility of stored data is reduced.

All of these problems of fragmentation stem from limitations on information-handling capacity. Advances made in information technology enhance the organization's ability to process information, and therefore permit it to get by with a lesser degree of fragmentation of the information system. These advances lead, in short, to increased integration of the information system.

---

[33] Hierarchical fragmentation of the data base, in which higher-level files contain summary information pertaining to lower-level files, tends to reduce the extent of duplicate storage. This concept is exemplified by accounting systems with journals of original entry, subsidiary ledgers, and general and control ledgers.

The extreme case of an integrated information system is one organized around a common data base. In such a system, collected data are stored in an appropriate section of the data base, where they are then accessible to all (authorized) parts of the organization. The output from any subsystem is likewise made generally available through the data base. Thus, the data base serves as a common depository of information for the entire organization, permitting a closer coupling of its activities.

It should be pointed out that the data base, though logically common to the entire organization, would normally still be physically fragmented. Fragmentation occurs, for instance, when portions of the data base are assigned to different levels in the hierarchy of physical storage media. Portions of the data base may also be geographically separated from other parts when, for example, certain data are used only at a remote location. The central portion of the data base should normally contain summary or abstracted data pertaining to the decentralized portions, consistent with the degree of centralized coordination required.[34]

Closer Coupling of Organizational Activities

It is important to distinguish between the information system and the organization it serves. Both constitute systems, and both involve a tradeoff between independence and integration. However, the motivation in integrating the parts of the information system is greater effectiveness in data processing, whereas integration of organizational activities is concerned with the effectiveness of the entire organization.

Integration of the information system is a necessary, but not sufficient, condition for integration of organizational activities. A closer coupling of these activities requires planning that covers a broader scope. This means that the planning must encompass more variables and must take into account more of the interactions among subunits of the organization. The information system must therefore be capable of (1) providing ready access to data about a wide range of activities; and (2) performing the complex processing required to achieve comprehensive planning.

This is not the appropriate place to amplify the discussion of integrated planning. The nature of the problem was introduced in the previous two chapters and is covered extensively in Chapter 5.

---

[34] The common data base concept is discussed in the following issues of *EDP Analyzer:* August 1966, November 1966, and December 1966.

CHAPTER 4

Economics of Information

INFORMATION is an economic resource available to the organization, and, like all such resources, it has a value and a cost. It also exhibits the well-known phenomenon of a declining marginal value: beyond a certain point, increases in information yield reduced net returns. The organization is naturally interested in designing an "optimal" information system in which the value of information is just balanced by its cost. Although in practice this point can at best only be approximated, it is worthwhile to discuss the issues involved.

Information is the raw material for the decision processes that govern the behavior of the organization. For all practical purposes, such behavior depends not so much on an objective reality as on the representation of reality contained in the data base of the organization (Boyd and Krasnow, 1963). One would hope, of course, that this representation is not wholly at odds with reality; but one should also recognize that the data base provides at best an extremely abstract and imperfect analogue of the real world.[1]

Information derives its value from the effect it has on the behavior of the organization. In order for new information to have value, (1) it must affect the existing analogue representation of the real world contained in the data base; (2) any change in the representation must then affect the decisions made as a function of the data base; and (3) an increase must occur in the utility derived as a result of changed decisions. Information thus has value only if it changes the organization's formal view of the world, if decisions are sensitive to such a change, and if utility is sensitive to differences in decisions. The incremental value of information is the utility achieved with the information, minus the utility that would have been obtained in the absence of the information. The information should of course be obtained if its incremental value exceeds its incremental cost.

4.1 *A Theoretical Model*[2]

A model will be used to illustrate these concepts. The model is based primarily on the work of J. Marschak (1954, 1959a, 1959b, 1962, 1963) (and amplified by Ying, 1964). We shall assume that the real world can be described in terms of discrete variables. The assumption of discreteness is justified on the grounds that variables can be measured and described with only finite resolution.

Payoff Matrix

Let x_i be a particular *state of nature* out of the set X of m recognized states,[3] where m is finite (though possibly immense). Each x_i is a vector

---

[1] Because of the abstract nature of data base information, it should normally be supplemented by direct contact with the real world. Direct observation by a planner can be viewed largely as a means of obtaining a (very sparse) sample of the real world in order to verify and improve the data base analogue.

[2] Sections 4.1 and 4.2 are relatively mathematical and can be skipped without seriously hampering understanding of later material.

[3] A "recognized" state is one that has been explicitly identified as a potential condition that can exist over the time period relevant to a given decision. The set X, therefore, will, in general, include only a small fraction of the "real" set of potential states. The states not included may be those that have an insignificant probability of occurring or those that have simply been overlooked.

(that is, multidimensional) quantity and represents an ensemble of detailed environmental variables, such as a demand schedule for each product, a supply schedule of resources, competitors' actions, and so forth. Irrelevant or unchanging aspects of states of nature can be ignored; only those variables that describe relevant and varying aspects need be stated explicitly. Decisions can then be made under the assumption that unstated aspects remain constant.

Similarly, let A be the set of recognized actions available to the organization, and let a_k be a particular action. Like the x_i, a given a_k is a vector that describes all of the detailed actions taken—production schedules, pricing decisions, the acquisition of resources, and the like. The set of actions might also include "doing nothing" (that is, continue doing what is currently being done) or the action of generating additional recognized states or alternative strategies. For convenience, we can ignore each *dominated* strategy that is either inferior or equal to some given alternative strategy for every state of nature. Suppose that s recognized actions exist.

For each recognized act–state pair (a_k, x_i) we shall asume that the organization is able to assign a payoff or utility, u_{ki}. The relationship can be displayed in the form of the well-known *payoff matrix, ω*.

State of Nature

Action		x_1	$\cdots$	x_i	$\cdots$	x_m
	a_1	u_{11}	$\cdots$	u_{1i}	$\cdots$	u_{1m}
	$\vdots$	$\vdots$		$\vdots$		$\vdots$
	a_k	u_{k1}	$\cdots$	u_{ki}	$\cdots$	u_{km}
	$\vdots$	$\vdots$		$\vdots$		$\vdots$
	a_s	u_{s1}	$\cdots$	u_{si}	$\cdots$	u_{sm}

Payoff Matrix, $[u_{ki}]$

The payoff matrix represents a model of reality. It provides the same sort of information that one typically can obtain from analytical or simulation models, but in a very much less compressed form than most. Each utility value shown in the matrix purports to measure, in terms of a single index, all of the multidimensional consequences stemming from a given action taken in the presence of a given state of nature. Utilities reflect, among other things, the organization's attitude toward risk taking.

The choice of which acts and states to include in a payoff matrix depends strongly on the level of decision being made. In the case of high-level decisions, the x_i and a_k typically cover a wide scope of states and actions, but each is described in terms of highly aggregated variables. Lower-level decisions are constrained (by higher-level decisions) to a much narrower scope, but the alternative actions and states of nature are described in considerably greater detail.

The specification of states of nature, alternative actions, and utilities crucially affects the behavior of the organization. An unrecognized state of nature or alternative action might just as well not exist. As a result, a decision maker may choose an action that has disastrous consequences if an unanticipated state of nature occurs, or he may fail to select an action with much more desirable consequences than any of the alternatives included in the set A. Similarly, perceived utilities may not correspond to the real utilities of the organization, especially if the decision maker's utilities represent subjective local goals derived imperfectly from the organization's global goals. One of the marks of the outstanding decision maker is his ability to generate a good set of states of nature and actions; and a necessary characteristic of a good planning system is its ability to induce decision makers to assign local utilities in reasonable conformity with global utilities.

Information Structure

The state of nature that will prevail during the time span affected by an action is not known with certainty. There are two reasons for this.

First, an action takes a finite time to implement, and its effects are then felt for some length of time. Accordingly, the relevant states of nature to be considered in the perceived payoff matrix are *future* states of nature. There thus exists an inherent uncertainty about the x_i.

Second, states of nature are perceived only indirectly through an information system. This system is subject to varying degrees of error, delay, and compression. As a result, the *existing* state of nature—and, *a fortiori,* the *future* state—is known imperfectly.

The information available about predicted future states of nature depends on the *structure* of the information system. The system provides information in the form of a *message* y_j, from a set Y of n potential messages, that gives an abstract representation of the predicted state of nature. The structure is defined in terms of q_{ij}, the conditional probability that the message y_j will be received if state x_i prevails.

The information structure Q can be displayed in matrix form:

Message

		y_1	$\cdots$	y_j	$\cdots$	y_n
	x_1	q_{11}	$\cdots$	q_{1j}	$\cdots$	q_{1n}
State	$\vdots$	$\vdots$		$\vdots$		$\vdots$
of	x_i	q_{i1}	$\cdots$	q_{ij}	$\cdots$	q_{in}
Nature	$\vdots$	$\vdots$		$\vdots$		$\vdots$
	x_m	q_{m1}	$\cdots$	q_{mj}	$\cdots$	q_{mn}

Information Structure, $Q[q_{ij}]$, where $q_{ij} = $ Prob $(y_j \mid x_i)$

If the information system provides a perfect correspondence between recognized states of nature and messages, the structure is defined by a unit matrix—that is, a matrix consisting solely of l's along its major diagonal.[4] Imperfect structures are defined by other than a unit matrix. Imperfections of the system arise in two ways. First, the structure may fail to differentiate between different states of nature; and second, messages may be subject to random errors.

In order to illustrate the first of these imperfections, consider the matrix on page 71. This information structure partitions the set of m states of X into n subsets (where typically n is much smaller than m). A single message y_j is associated with the subset $x_t, \ldots, x_u$, and thus the information system does not differentiate between these states.

If the number of potential messages is much less than the number of states, each message provides less information (in terms of information theory) than it would if no compression took place. But compression, in the form, say, of aggregating detailed data, has the very desirable effect of reducing information handling within the system. However, it will also, in general, reduce expected payoff. In the extreme case, the structure Q is represented by an $m \times 1$ matrix in which only one potential message exists. Such a structure, like a shepherd who only cries "wolf," provides no information about the state of nature.

If the information system fails to distinguish between states of nature that yield different payoffs for at least one of the alternative actions, the information structure is then said to be *too coarse*. If, on the other hand, it

---

[4] Or, equivalently, any matrix derived from the interchange of rows or columns of a unit matrix.

Message

y_1 y_2 y_3 $\cdots$ y_j $\cdots$ y_n

	y_1	y_2	y_3	y_j	y_n
x_1	1				
x_2	1				
$\vdots$	$\vdots$				
x_r	1				
x_{r+1}		1			
$\vdots$		$\vdots$			
x_s		1			
x_{s+1}			1		
$\vdots$			$\vdots$		
x_t				1	
$\vdots$				$\vdots$	
x_u				1	
$\vdots$					$\vdots$
x_m					1

State of Nature (row labels at left)

Information Structure

differentiates between states having identical payoffs for all actions, the structure is *too fine*. It is *payoff relevant* if it is neither too coarse nor too fine (Marschak, 1963). A structure may be simultaneously too fine and too coarse if the partitioning effected by the structure is neither a subpartitioning nor an aggregation of payoff-relevant partitioning. Because one typically does not know what the payoff-relevant partitioning is, information structures are, in general, both too fine and too coarse. The different cases are illustrated in Figure 4-1.

The set of actions A can be similarly partitioned, and the structure Q may be too coarse, too fine, or payoff relevant with respect to this partitioning. A necessary and sufficient condition for Q to be payoff relevant with respect to each act–state pair is that it be payoff relevant separately with respect to the partitioning of X and A (Marschak, 1963, pp. 720–721).

In addition to the distortions caused by partitioning, the information structure also suffers from another type of imperfection: the (condensed) prediction of the state of nature that it provides is, in general, subject to random errors. Consequently, when a message is received the decision maker cannot place complete reliance on it. As a result the message has a lower information content than it would if the information channel were perfectly deterministic. In the polar case in which all messages have an

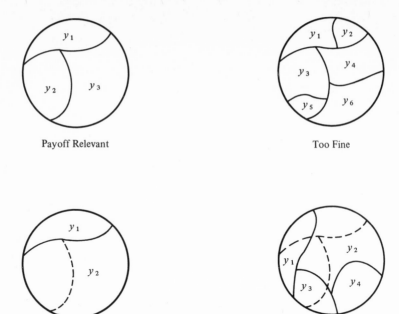

Payoff Relevant

Too Fine

Too Coarse

Too Fine and Too Coarse

Figure 4-1. Alternative partitioning of states of nature by the information structure

equal probability of occurring regardless of the state of nature (that is, if $q_{ij} = 1/n$ for all i and j), a message provides no additional information.

Prior and Posterior Information About States of Nature

Included in the data base of the organization should be data useful for predicting future states of nature. This information is embodied in the form of *prior* probability estimates. Let p_i be the prior probability that state x_i will prevail over the time span relevant to the current decision, and let P be the vector $(p_1, p_2, \ldots, p_m)$.

Information is received about x_i in the form of a message y_j. The probability r_j of receiving message y_j can be calculated as follows:

$$r_j = \text{Prob}(y_j) = \sum_i \text{Prob}(y_j \mid x_i) \cdot \text{Prob}(x_i) = \sum_i q_{ij} \cdot p_i \quad \text{(Eq. 1)}$$

The receipt of message j will, in general, alter the decision maker's view of the world and cause him to revise his estimates of state probabilities. The revised estimates constitute *posterior* probabilities. The posterior estimates can be calculated through a Bayesian analysis.[5] Now,

[5] See, for example, Schlaifer (1961).

$$\text{Prob}\,(x_i \mid y_j) \cdot \text{Prob}\,(y_j) = \text{Prob}\,(x_i, y_j) = \text{Prob}\,(y_j \mid x_i) \cdot \text{Prob}\,(x_i)$$

Letting $\bar{p}_{ij} = \text{Prob}\,(x_i \mid y_j)$,

$$\bar{p}_{ij} = \frac{\text{Prob}\,(y_j \mid x_i) \cdot \text{Prob}\,(x_i)}{\text{Prob}\,(y_j)} = \frac{q_{ij} \cdot p_i}{r_j} \qquad \begin{aligned} i &= 1, 2, \ldots, m \\ j &= 1, 2, \ldots, n \end{aligned} \qquad \text{(Eq. 2)}$$

The $\bar{p}_{ji}$ are based on more information than the p_i (since they take into account message y_j), and so the former are used in decision making. The great virtue of this Bayesian approach is that it allows the decision maker to make improved inferences about the state of nature whenever additional environmental information becomes available.

Choice of Action

Suppose the decision maker receives the message y_j. Which action a_k should he choose? Under these circumstances, he perceives the expected value of the kth action to be

$$U(a_k, y_j) = U_{kj} = \sum_i \bar{p}_{ij} u_{ki} \qquad \text{(Eq. 3)}$$

If his object is to maximize expected utility,[6] he should choose the action $\hat{a}_j$ that maximizes U_{kj}:

$$U(\hat{a}_j, y_j) = \hat{U}_j = \max_k U_{kj} \qquad \text{(Eq. 4)}$$

Value of Information

A message provides information because it selects a given y_j out of the set Y of potential messages. Its value derives from the fact that one does not know *with certainty* which y_j will be received.[7] In assessing the value of a given information structure one must estimate (either explicitly or implicitly) the prior probability of receiving each of the potential messages.

---

[6] This is a reasonable decision, but others have also been proposed. Wald's "maximin" criterion, for example, is one that maximizes the minimum utility that can be achieved regardless of which state of nature occurs. Savage proposes a similar criterion of choosing the action that minimaxes "regret," where regret is defined as the difference between the optimum utility for a given state of nature and the utility actually received. In general, such criteria will not lead to the action that maximizes long-run expected utility. Miller and Starr (1960, pp. 55–98) discuss these issues.

[7] A message may have value, however, if it only confirms what one strongly suspected in advance. But its value approaches zero as the probability of correctly predicting the message approaches 1. See page 85–86.

The estimated frequency of receiving message y_j, based on prior probabilities, is $\sum_i p_i q_{ij}$. Let us call this probability r_j. Therefore, the expected utility V with prior information P and information structure Q can be calculated by[8]

$$V(P, Q) = \sum_j r_j \hat{U}_j \qquad \text{(Eq. 5)}$$

A given information structure should be valued on an incremental basis. In other words, the value of information structure Q equals utility $V(P, Q)$ minus the maximum expected utility that could be achieved with no (additional) information. Thus, in evaluating a structure, one should assess the available prior information and choose an appropriate decision process that most fully exploits such information.

Let $V(P_o, Q_o)$ be the expected utility that would be achieved using the optimum decision process based on the absence of additional information. Without additional information the expected payoff from action k is

$$U_{ko} = \sum_i p_i u_{ki} \qquad \text{(Eq. 6)}$$

Therefore,

$$V_o = \max_k U_{ko} \qquad \text{(Eq. 7)}$$

The expected incremental value of the additional information ΔV is simply the difference between V and V_o:

$$\Delta V = V - V_o \qquad \text{(Eq. 8)}$$

It is on this estimated value ΔV that the one should base the design of the optimal information structure.

Figure 4-2 shows the calculation of ΔV in the form of a flow diagram (based on Blanning, 1967).

---

[8] In order to determine a single (cardinal) measure for the value of information, it is necessary that the u_{ki} (and thus the $\hat{U}_j$) provide single cardinal measures of utility. However, the u_{ki} can also be thought of as vector quantities, in which the elements represent cardinal measures of incommensurable payoff dimensions (such as accounting profit, corporate "image," rate of growth, and the like). In this case, the value of information is also a vector quantity—namely, the change along each payoff dimension that results from the availability of the information.

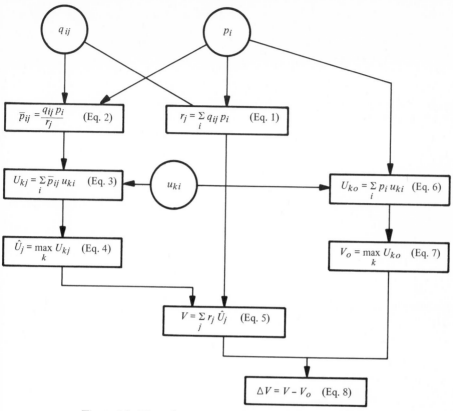

Figure 4-2. Flow diagram of information value calculations

The true (post hoc) expected incremental value of a given structure will, in general, differ from the prior estimate. The prior estimate is a function of the perceived payoff matrix and the prior probability estimates, whereas the true expected payoff depends on the (unknown) true payoff matrix ω', information structure Q', and state probabilities P'. Matrix ω' has the same structure as the perceived payoff matrix ω, but is based on the true utility achieved, u'_{ki}, when action a_k is taken when the true state x'_i prevails. Thus,

$$V'(P, Q) = \sum_j r'_j \sum_i \omega'(\hat{a}_j, x'_i),$$

where V' is the true gross value of structure Q and r'_j is the real probability of receiving message j. The true incremental value of information therefore equals

$$\Delta V' = V'(P, Q) - V'(P_o, Q_o)$$

Information can increase payoff (and hence have a positive value[9]) in two different ways: (1) it can improve the choice of actions based on the existing perceived payoff matrix and prior probability estimates; or (2) it can assist the decision maker in recognizing additional relevant states of nature, generating improved actions, developing a more realistic utility function, and making more accurate estimates of the prior probabilities.

These latter improvements are a more fundamental or "higher-level" nature than the former. But they are also much less susceptible to formal analysis, since they involve a search for information of a character essentially unknown to the decision maker. For this reason, the organization typically establishes exploratory information channels—for example, market-research groups, operations-research staffs, personal inspection trips by managers, and the like—to probe for improved information for which no current precise requirement is recognized (but obviously with the expectation that the resulting value of the information will exceed its cost).

4.2 *An Example*

The concepts brought out by the theoretical model can be made clearer by use of a numerical example. Suppose there exist four similar pieces of material, M_1, M_2, M_3, and M_4, all of which have the same prior probability p of being defective. Suppose further that there are four items, I_1, I_2, I_3, and I_4, any one of which can be produced from any nondefective piece of material (defective material cannot be used to produce any of the items). Only one unit of each item is needed; any more than that is useless. Let V_i be the value of a good unit of the ith item. Defective units have zero value.

Let us assume that the manufacturing process is such that a given piece of material, once assigned to a given item, is irrevocably committed. A defective piece is not detected until after the process has begun. If a piece proves defective, the item for which it is intended cannot be completed satisfactorily. It is, however, possible to assign more than one piece of

---

[9] If the decision maker receives and acts on "bad" information (in the sense that posterior information is less accurate than prior information), it may decrease payoff and hence have a negative value. Presumably, the decision maker would soon abandon a message source that continually gives what he perceives to be poor estimates of states. Even when posterior probability estimates are "good" (in the sense that they give the correct relative frequencies of states over a large number of decision cycles), the action with the highest expected utility may prove on hindsight to be a poorer choice than the one that would have been taken if only prior information had been available.

material to the same item in order to achieve a higher probability of being able to produce (at least) one good unit. The assignment of pieces must be made at the beginning of the production period. Item due dates and manufacturing lead times preclude sequential decisions that defer the allocation of some pieces until the quality is known of pieces previously put into production. The problem is to choose an assignment of material to items in a way that maximizes total value.

Since there are four pieces of material, each of which may be either good or defective, there exist 2^4, or 16, different states of nature. If "G" stands for good and "D" for defective, each possible state can be represented by a vector having G's or D's as elements:

State of Nature

	x_0	x_1	x_2	x_3	x_4	x_5	x_6	x_7	x_8	x_9	x_{10}	x_{11}	x_{12}	x_{13}	x_{14}	x_{15}
M_1	G	G	G	G	G	G	G	G	D	D	D	D	D	D	D	D
M_2	G	G	G	G	D	D	D	D	G	G	G	G	D	D	D	D
M_3	G	G	D	D	G	G	D	D	G	G	D	D	G	G	D	D
M_4	G	D	G	D	G	D	G	D	G	D	G	D	G	D	G	D

Material

Table of Potential States of Nature

Alternative actions can be outlined similarly. Since any piece of material can be assigned to any one of four products, there exists a total of 4^4, or 256, different assignments. One action would be to assign all material to item 1, another action would be to assign all to item 2, and so on. A partial table of alternative actions is shown below.

Action

	a_1	a_2	a_3	$\cdots$	a_{255}	a_{256}
M_1	I_1	I_1	I_1	$\cdots$	I_3	I_4
M_2	I_1	I_1	I_1	$\cdots$	I_4	I_4
M_3	I_1	I_1	I_2	$\cdots$	I_4	I_4
M_4	I_1	I_2	I_2	$\cdots$	I_4	I_4

Material

Table of Alternative Assignments

Let us consider a specific example. Suppose that both the real and perceived indices of value are $V_1 = 60$, $V_2 = 20$, $V_3 = 10$, and $V_4 = 10$. The decision maker is then in a position to construct a payoff matrix. In doing this, it will be possible for him to reduce the number of alternative actions to be considered, since many of the actions are dominated by at least one other action. For example, since V_1 exceeds all other V_i, the action of assigning all material to item 1 dominates the actions that assign all material to any other single item. In fact, one can reject any action that assigns more material to I_2, I_3, or I_4 than to I_1. On similar grounds, actions can be rejected that assign more material to I_3 or I_4 than to I_2. There remain a total of 47 alternative actions after the dominated actions have been eliminated.

A 16×47 payoff matrix can be constructed for this example. If, say, state of nature x_0 prevails (that is, all pieces good), and one piece of material is assigned to each item, a total value of 100 will be achieved. The table shown below shows a portion of the payoff matrix.[10]

State of Nature

		x_0 (GGGG)	x_1 (GGGD)	x_2 (GGDG)	$\cdots$	x_{14} (DDDG)	x_{15} (DDDD)
	a_1 (1111)	60	60	60	$\cdots$	60	0
	a_2 (1112)	80	60	80	$\cdots$	20	0
Action	a_3 (1121)	80	80	60	$\cdots$	60	0
	$\vdots$	$\vdots$	$\vdots$	$\vdots$	$\vdots$	$\vdots$	$\vdots$
	a_{47} (4321)	100	40	80	$\cdots$	60	0

Payoff Matrix

Payoff in the Absence of Prior Probability Estimates

Suppose that the decision maker only has information about the (real) payoff matrix. That is, he has no prior information about the probability of defective p, and receives no additional information about the state of nature. Under these circumstances, he has no basis for choosing the action that maximizes expected payoff. He must therefore resort to some other decision criterion.

[10] The notation $(ijkl)$ used in the table has the following meaning: For actions (where i, j, k, and l can equal 1, 2, 3, or 4), it signifies the assignment of piece 1 to product i, piece 2 to product j, and so forth. For example, action (1121) means that pieces 1, 2, and 4 are assigned to product 1 and piece 3 is assigned to product 2. The notation for states of nature (where i, j, k, and l can equal G or D) signifies that piece 1 is in condition i, piece 2 is in condition j, etc. For example (GGGD) means that pieces 1, 2, and 3 are good and piece 4 is defective.

The *maximin*[11] criterion suggests the selection of action a_1, the assignment of all pieces to item 1, since a value of 60 will be achieved for all states of nature except the one with four defectives (which yields zero value regardless of action). This also happens to be the strategy dictated by the criterion of minimizing maximum regret. Although the suitability of these decision criteria may be open to serious questions, for the time being we shall accept the assignment of all pieces to item 1 as the appropriate one in the case where no information (except the payoff matrix ω) is available to the decision maker.

The actual payoff achieved as a result of this strategy depends on the actual state of nature revealed during the production process. The expected payoff $V(P_o, Q_o)$ equals $60(1 - p^4) + 0p^4$, where p is the probability that a given piece is defective. For example, when p equals .5, the expected payoff is 56.25 units.

Payoff with Complete Information

We are now in a position to determine the value of acquiring additional information. Consider the polar case in which the decision maker has complete information about the state of nature. The information structure in this case consists of a 16×16 unit matrix, which we shall call Q_C. With such a structure, the decision maker knows precisely the condition of each piece at the time he makes material assignments. This might be realized in practice, for example, through the development of a test procedure that determines prior to processing which pieces of material are good and which are defective.

The obvious action under these circumstances is to assign the good pieces in the order I_1, I_2, I_3, and I_4, until they are exhausted. The payoff achieved depends on the number of defective pieces. The following tabulation shows the value under different conditions:

Number of defective pieces:	0	1	2	3	4
Value:	100	90	80	60	0

The expected (gross) value of perfect information therefore depends on the real probability p that any given piece is defective. By the binomial probability law, the probability $P(d)$ of having d defective pieces is specified by the probability mass function

---

[11] See footnote 6, page 73.

$$P(d) = \frac{4!}{4!(4-d)!}\, p^d(1-p)^{4-d}$$

Therefore, the expected absolute payoff with perfect information is calculated by the following formula:[12]

$$V(P, Q_C) = 100 \cdot 1(1-p)^4 + 90 \cdot 4p(1-p)^3 + 80 \cdot 6p^2(1-p)^2$$
$$+ 60 \cdot 4p^3(1-p) + 0 \cdot 1p^4$$

The incremental value of perfect information equals $V(P, Q_C) - V(P_0, Q_0)$. If p equals .5, the expected gross payoff with perfect information is 73.75. Therefore, the incremental value of perfect information is 73.75 − 56.25, or 17.50 units, an increase of 31 per cent over the expected payoff when only the payoff matrix is known.

Payoff with Known Prior Probability of Defective and Zero State Information

The two preceding cases provide a lower and upper limit on the expected value of information.[13] We can now discuss the more typical cases of decision making under partial information. Suppose, for example, that the decision maker has an accurate prior estimate of the real probability of having a defective, but that he receives no additional information about the actual state of nature. In this case he must select in advance the assignment of each piece, and he has no opportunity to revise these assignments.

The decision maker must select one of five (nondominated) actions:

Action	Assignment	
a_1	1111	(Maximin strategy)
a_2	1112	
a_3	1122	
a_4	1123	
a_5	1234	

[12] Precisely the same value is found from Equation 5, in which r_j (the probability of receiving message j and hence—with perfect information—being in state j) equals $p^d(1-p)^{4-d}$. With the complete information structure, prior information about probability p adds no additional information.

[13] We could have taken the case of the complete absence of information, including knowledge of the payoff matrix, as the lowest limit. This would simply have changed

Since nothing is known in advance about the state of the individual pieces, it is immaterial which piece is assigned to which of the items. Thus, the expected payoff of strategy 1122, say, is the same as for strategies 1212, 1221, and so on.

The optimal strategy $\hat{a}_j$ is determined from Equation 4.[14] It obviously depends on the estimated value of the prior probability of defective (which in the present example is also the posterior probability, since no new information is received). This is shown in the following table.

Range of p	Optimal Action
.00000– .16667	a_5, 1234
.16667– .40825	a_4, 1123
.40825– .69333	a_2, 1112
.69333–1.00000	a_1, 1111

Notice that the maximin action corresponds to the optimal action when the probability of defective is greater than .69333. Thus, the choice of the maximin action does, in fact, imply a knowledge of the prior probability of defective—namely, it implies that it exceeds .69333 (Starr 1964, p. 164).

The expected payoff naturally declines with increasing values of p, as shown in Figure 4-3. This figure shows the expected payoff both with complete information and with only knowledge of the real value of p. The payoff resulting from each of the five alternative actions is plotted.[15] The heavy line represents the expected payoff from the optimum action; it is simply composed of segments of the individual action curves that have the highest expected value within each range of p.

The incremental value of accurate prior information is the difference between the optimal expected payoff with the information and the expected value achieved with the maximin strategy. When p has the known value of

---

the base value of information and would have raised the unnecessary issue of how one makes a decision with no information about payoffs or states of nature.

[14] The expected value of each action can also be calculated directly. For example, the expected value of action a_2, 1112, equals $60(1 - p^3) + 20(1 - p)$. Similar expressions can be used for the other four actions.

[15] From Figure 4-3 it can be observed that strategy a_2 is probably superior to the maximin strategy a_1, since the former may yield a considerably higher payoff than the latter and cannot be much worse. This illustrates the fact that the minimaxing criterion is usually not very appropriate.

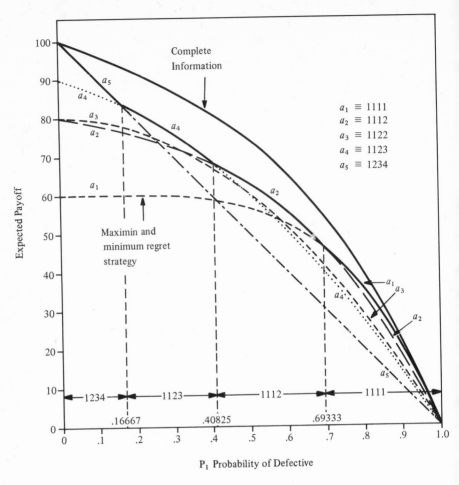

Figure 4-3. Expected payoff of alternative actions

.5, the expected value is 62.50. This yields an incremental value of 6.25, or a gain of 11.11 per cent over the maximin strategy.

Payoff with Known Prior Probability and Partial State Information

Any additional information about the actual state of nature will increase the expected payoff. Suppose, for example, that a means exists for testing the condition of a piece of material, but the cost of the test is high enough that we are interested in limiting its use. We might consider, for example, testing only two of the four pieces. If we test pieces 1 and 2 (the choice of which two is immaterial), this scheme is equivalent to the following coarse information structure:

Message

		y_1	y_2	y_3	y_4
x_0	GGGG	1			
x_1	GGGD	1			
x_2	GGDG	1			
x_3	GGDD	1			
x_4	GDGG		1		
x_5	GDGD		1		
x_6	GDDG		1		
x_7	GDDD		1		
x_8	DGGG			1	
x_9	DGGD			1	
x_{10}	DGDG			1	
x_{11}	DGDD			1	
x_{12}	DDGG				1
x_{13}	DDGD				1
x_{14}	DDDG				1
x_{15}	DDDD				1

State of Nature

Information Structure, Test of Items 1 and 2

With such information, the decision maker maximizes expected payoff if he uses the following decision rule:

Message	Action	
y_1	1234[16]	
y_2	$\begin{cases} 1X22 \\ 1X23 \text{ or } 1X24 \end{cases}$	if $p > \frac{1}{2}$ otherwise
y_3	$\begin{cases} X122 \\ X123 \text{ or } X124 \end{cases}$	if $p > \frac{1}{2}$ otherwise
y_4	$\begin{cases} XX11 \\ XX12 \end{cases}$	if $p > \frac{1}{3}$ otherwise

This rule yields an expected payoff of 71.25 when $p = .5$. The incremental value over the minimax strategy is therefore $71.25 - 56.25$, or 15.00 units (compared with an incremental value for perfect information of 17.50 units).

The incremental value of coarse information provided by partial testing depends on both the degree of coarseness (that is, the number of tests performed) and the (known) prior probability of defective p. Figure 4-4

[16] As before, this notation means that piece 1 is assigned to item 1, piece 2 to item 2, etc. An "X" stands for a discarded defective unit.

shows the incremental value of information, using as a base the case in which the prior probability p is known. The figure shows the values of three alternative structures corresponding to one, two, and three tests with a known prior probability.[17] (A fourth test does not add to value, because the untested material can simply be assigned to the item with the highest remaining value after all tested good material has been assigned in descending value sequence.)

The figure displays the rather obvious fact that an increase in relevant information results in a higher expected utility. However, incremental in-

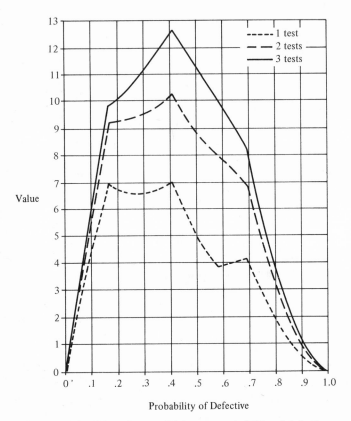

Figure 4-4. Value of tests with known probability of defective

[17] Kinks appear in Figure 4-4 (as well as some of the ones that follow) because of the discrete nature of the problem. For example, at $p = .40825$ the optimal action shifts from a_4 to a_2, causing an abrupt change in the slope of the payoff curve at this point.

formation in general yields declining incremental utility. The following table shows the incremental value of each test when p is .5.

Test	Value Achieved	Incremental Value of Test
1st	5.00	5.00
2nd	8.75	3.75
3rd	11.25	2.50
4th	11.25	.00

The goal of balancing the cost and value of information leads to the following decision rule[18] when p is .5:

$$5.00 \leq \text{cost of test} \qquad\qquad : \text{Perform 0 test}$$
$$3.75 \leq \text{cost of test} < 5.00 : \text{Perform 1 test}$$
$$2.50 \leq \text{cost of test} < 3.75 : \text{Perform 2 tests}$$
$$0 \quad \leq \text{cost of test} < 2.50 : \text{Perform 3 tests}$$
$$\text{cost of test} < 0 \qquad : \text{Perform 4 tests}$$

The probability of having a defective strongly affects the value of information. If no test data are available but p is known to be near zero, the decision maker should assign one piece of material to each of the four items. If a test is performed and it reveals that a piece is good, then no change is made in the decision that would have been made in the absence of the data. In such a case, then, the test contributed no value. But with a p near zero, most tests will only confirm what was otherwise strongly suspected—in other words, posterior information will in most cases be the same as prior information. Therefore, the incremental value of test data is quite small.

For similar reasons, the value of information also declines as p approaches one. A known value of p near one makes it easy to predict material quality and choose an assignment in the absence of additional information: most of the pieces will be defective, and therefore they should all be assigned to item 1. Additional information therefore provides few surprises and offers little incremental payoff. This is simply another illus-

[18] If a test reveals that a piece is defective, the production cost for that piece can be avoided. The expected value of the savings equals p times the unit production cost. The net cost of a test equals its gross cost minus the expected production savings.

tration of the general principle that additional information about the existing state of nature declines in value as nature becomes more predictable.

The table below summarizes the incremental value of tests when p
equals .05, .50, or .95.

Incremental Value of Test

Test	$p = .05$	$p = .50$	$p = .95$
1st	2.37	5.00	1.43
2nd	.57	3.75	.095
3rd	.05	2.50	.0475
4th	.00	.00	.00

Payoff with Known Prior Probability and a Noisy Information Structure

The examples discussed so far assume that the message associated with
a given predicted state of nature is received with certainty—that is,

$$q_{ij} = \begin{cases} 1 \text{ for some unique } j \\ 0 \text{ for all other } j \end{cases} \quad i = 1, 2, \ldots, m$$

This, of course, is an unrealistic assumption. Errors occur both in measuring
the existing state of nature and in predicting future states on the basis of
current information. These errors will, in general, lower expected payoff.

Suppose that all pieces are tested, but the test is subject to error. If a
piece is actually good, it will be reported as defective with error probability
p_e. For simplicity, we shall assume that a defective piece is reported as good
with this same probability. We also assume independence among errors.

For any given true state of nature there exists some probability that it
will be reported as a different state. For example, if the true state of nature
is $x_4 = $ GDGG (piece 2 defective, all the rest good), the message about the
state will be correct with probability $(1 - p_e)^4$, and hence will be erroneous
with probability $1 - (1 - p_e)^4$.

The probability that a given state will be reported as some different state
depends on the number of errors involved in the transformation between
the two states. For example, a single error is involved in reporting state x_4
as state $x_0 = $ GGGG or as state $x_5 = $ GDGD. The following table shows
the number of errors and their associated probability for each possible
transformation of state x_4.

Probability of a Reporting Error

Number of Errors	Reported State $y_j \mid x_4$	Probability q_{4j}	Probability of Error p_e			
			.1	.2	.3	.4
0	GDGG	$(1 - p_e)^4 = .6561$	.4096	.2401	.1296	
1	DDGG, GGGG, GDDG, GDGD	$P_e(1 - p_e)^3 = .0729$	.1024	.1029	.0864	
2	DGGG, DDDG, DDGD, GGDG, GGGD, GDDD	$P_e^2(1 - p_e)^2 = .0081$	.0256	.0441	.0576	
3	DGDG, DGGD, DDDD, GGDD	$P_e^3(1 - p_e) = .0009$	.0064	.0189	.0384	
4	DGDD	$p_e^{\check{}} = .0001$	.0016	.0081	.0256	

The polar case of $p_e = 0$ corresponds to the structure providing complete information. When $p_e = .5$, all $q_{ij} = .5^4 = .0625 = \frac{1}{16}$, and therefore a message does not provide any information at all about the state of nature. This corresponds, of course, to the earlier example in which only the prior probability of defective is known.

Figure 4-5 shows the expected incremental value of "noisy" information, using as the base the expected payoff when only the value of p (in addition to the payoff matrix) is known. As can be seen, the value of information decreases as it becomes increasingly subject to error. A decision based on an erroneous message leads, in general, to a payoff less than would have been possible with a correct message. The reduction in expected payoff depends on the frequency of errors, the extent of the errors (that is, the degree of discrepancy between the actual and reported state of nature), and the sensitivity of payoff to changes in the predicted state of nature.

Payoff with Errors in Estimate of Prior Probability

All the previous examples (except the one discussed in connection with the maximin strategy) assume that the decision maker knows the real prior probability of having a defective. But suppose such information is not known with certainty. Let us examine the sensitivity of payoff to errors in estimating p.

Clearly, a decision based on an erroneous estimate of p will, in general, not be the optimal decision. The foregone opportunity sustained from taking a nonoptimal decision represents the value of a perfect estimate of p. It depends on three factors. First, it depends on the sensitivity of posterior probabilities to errors in prior probabilities. If the information structure provides reliable and sufficiently fine information about the states of nature,

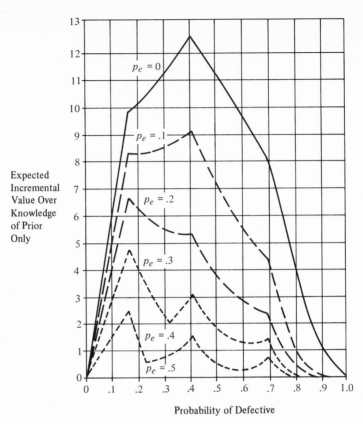

Figure 4-5. Expected incremental value of information
subject to error

the decision process is relatively insensitive to errors in prior probabilities. It can be seen from Equation 1, for example, that if the structure provides complete information (for example, $q_{ij} = 1$ if and only if $i = j$), posterior probability $\bar{p}_{ij}$ equals q_{ij} and therefore does not depend at all on the prior probabilities p_i. On the other hand, as all q_{ij} approach $1/n$, $\bar{p}_{ij}$ approaches p_i. Thus, as one might expect, errors in the p_i have a greater effect when only prior information is available.

Second, the expected value of an improved estimate of p also depends on the sensitivity of decisions to changes in the posterior probabilities. If actions are discrete, as they are in the material-assignment examples, the optimal action does not change within a range of p. For example, in the case of decision making when the only information available is the value of p, the optimal action remains the same if p lies anywhere within the range 0–.16667. Therefore, if both the estimated and the true value of p lie within this range, no penalty is paid for any error in the estimate.

Finally, the value of improving p also depends on the sensitivity of expected payoff to changes in action. Typically, deviations from the optimal action exhibit a saucer-shaped loss function; only when the deviation is "large" does the loss become very significant. It can be seen from Figure 4-3, for example, that the difference is relatively small in the expected pay-offs between the optimum and a "near-optimum" strategy.

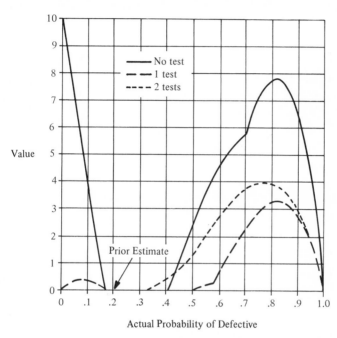

Figure 4-6. Value of accurate estimate of probability of defective when prior estimate equals .2

Figure 4-6 illustrates some of these concepts. The curves show the penalty, as a function of the true value of p, when p is erroneously estimated to equal .2. As can be seen, the penalty is in general greatest when no additional information is provided. As additional tests are performed, less reliance is placed on the prior estimate. However, decisions happen to be more sensitive to errors in estimating p with two tests than with one test, and so the value of better estimates is greater despite the reduced uncertainty.

4.3 Deficiencies in the Theoretical Model

The theoretical treatment of the economics of information obviously represents an abstraction. Like all abstractions, it does not portray reality perfectly. Perhaps the most serious imperfection is that it provides a static rather than a dynamic model, in that it does not explicitly consider the effects of accumulating information over several time periods in a repetitive decision process. The model suggests that information that does not lead to action can have no value. This is certainly true if the information *never* affects action, but information having no immediate value may make a contribution in subsequent periods. For example, new information may only confirm an uncertain prediction that could have been made without the information, but the reduction in uncertainty may lead to better predictions and hence higher utility for future decisions.

Quite apart from any theoretical limitations of the model, it is obviously difficult to apply in practice. In order to do this, one must first specify the information structure in terms of the probability matrix $[q_{ij}]$. That is, it is necessary to estimate the conditional probability of receiving a given message for each true state of nature. One must also estimate the prior probability associated with each state. Finally, the model requires the specification of a payoff matrix (or its equivalent in the form of a function).

Information of this sort is rarely available, particularly at the time one is assessing alternative information systems. For example, estimates of the q_{ij} typically can be made only after a given information structure has been implemented and some experience has been gained in its use. A systems designer thus faces the paradox that he must implement a given system before he can assess its value.

Estimating prior probabilities also presents great difficulty. Placing a value on information may require probability estimates for states outside the experience or control of the organization—such as the sales of an entirely new product, the cost of various resources, changes in laws (for example, taxes or import restrictions), and the actions of competitors (or opponents in the case of defense systems). A strong case can be made for forcing the organization to make explicit subjective probability estimates for such variables if they significantly affect decisions, but ordinarily this is most difficult to accomplish.

The need to completely formalize a decision process in order to place a value on information similarly restricts one's ability to quantify the value of information. A decision model must be available to determine the consequences of a given act and state of nature. The consequences must ultimately be expressed in the form of a cardinal utility function in order to measure the incremental effect of a given type of information. Such a high degree of formalization rarely exists, particularly in the case of higher-level decision processes.

Nevertheless, a theoretical discussion of the value of information has

considerable usefulness. First of all, substantial formalization is now possible, particularly in lower-level processes that deal with routine operations.
When some degree of formalization exists, various analyses can be under-
taken to provide some indication of the value of improved information. A
theoretical understanding of the issues involved can prove useful in doing
this.

Such an understanding should also provide managers and systems designers with a better insight into how information systems can be improved.
They should understand that information has value only if (1) expected
posterior probability estimates differ from prior estimates (that is, the information has some "surprise" content); (2) if decisions are sensitive to the
availability of additional information; and (3) if payoff is sensitive to differences in decisions. A greater appreciation of these principles would
probably have prevented some of the uneconomic information systems that
one finds all too often.

4.4 *Quantitative Analysis of Information Value*[19]

Despite the very limited possibility of placing an explicit value on a
given type of information, some quantification of the problem is often possible when partial formalization exists. Sensitivity analyses play a part in
any good operations research study, and these provide useful indications of
the value of information.

Parametric Analyses

Consider, for example, the application of a model for determining economic order quantities of inventory items.[20] The classical *EOQ* formula is

$$EOQ = \sqrt{\frac{2DR}{C}} \qquad \text{(Eq. 9)}$$

where D is the annual demand for an item, R is its reordering cost, and C
is its annual carrying cost per unit. Suppose we are interested in the effect
of an error in forecasting demand. If the forecast F is in error by a factor

[19] See Blanning (1967) for a more complete discussion of this topic.

[20] The example chosen somewhat simplifies the real problem of determining an
economic order quantity, since it ignores the related problem of determining the
order point. Goetz (1965, pp. 368–416) discusses these issues in considerable detail.

k, then from Equation 9 we can see that the calculated order quantity differs from the true *EOQ* by a factor of $\sqrt{k}$. That is, if $F = kD$, then

$$q = \sqrt{k}\, q_0$$

where q is the calculated order quantity with forecast F and q_0 is the true *EOQ*. Thus, an error in the forecast leads to a considerably smaller relative error in the calculated order quantity.

But that is not the full story. We are really interested in the cost penalty of the forecast error, and not order quantities *per se*. Total variable cost is calculated by the following function.[21]

$$TVC = \frac{q \cdot C}{2} + \frac{D}{2} \cdot R$$

From this it can be shown that

$$TVC = \frac{1}{2}\left(\sqrt{k} + \frac{1}{\sqrt{k}}\right) \cdot TVC_0$$

where TVC is the total annual variable cost resulting from forecast F which is in error by factor k, and TVC_0 is the total annual variable cost using true demand D.

The penalty factor, $\frac{1}{2}(\sqrt{k} + 1/\sqrt{k})$, has several relevant properties. When k equals 1 (and thus the forecast equals the true demand), the penalty factor also equals 1 and thus no penalty is suffered. Any value of k other than 1 results in a penalty factor greater than 1 (which is an obvious requirement, since a forecast error must lead to a cost greater than the minimum possible cost).

The analysis shows that the cost penalty is quite insensitive to forecast errors. This is so because (1) order quantity is fairly insensitive to forecast errors, and (2) cost is insensitive to deviations from the optimum order quantity. For example, a forecast of four times the true demand (that is, $k = 4$) results in an order quantity twice as large as the optimum quantity. This in turn results in a cost penalty of only 25 per cent. Figure 4-7 shows the penalty factor as a function of the forecast error. Figure 4-8 illustrates the same phenomenon with a specific example.

---

[21] This is obviously a simplification. It assumes a constant demand rate and neglects the cost of stockouts.

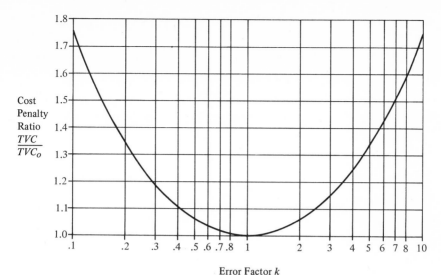

Error Factor k

Figure 4-7. Inventory cost penalty as a function of forecast errors

Of what value is such an analysis? Even though it does not place a value on a given information system (in this case a forecasting system), the analysis does serve a highly useful purpose. If it is known, for example, that the present system is capable of providing forecasts with an error parameter k ranging from $\frac{1}{4}$ to 4 (that is, 25 to 400 per cent of true demand), the analysis shows that variable inventory costs can be reduced by at most 25 per cent.

This may or may not exceed the cost of implementing a new forecasting model. If the cost exceeds 25 per cent, the new system can be rejected out of hand. If not, further analysis can be directed at refining the estimated improvement in forecasts in order to judge the possible benefits. In any event, analysis of the error penalty provides a systematic way of evaluating alternative forecasts for use in the inventory decision model.

Intervals of Insensitivity

Although inventory cost in the preceding example is quite insensitive to the forecast, it nevertheless varies continuously as a function of the error parameter k. In some situations payoff may be completely insensitive over certain intervals of data input values. Identification of those intervals provides important clues about the value of improving data inputs.

Consider, for example, the defective-material problem discussed earlier. Suppose that we have no means to test material prior to assignments. In Figure 4-3, it was shown that the optimal action does not change within intervals of p, the probability of having a defective. When p has a value

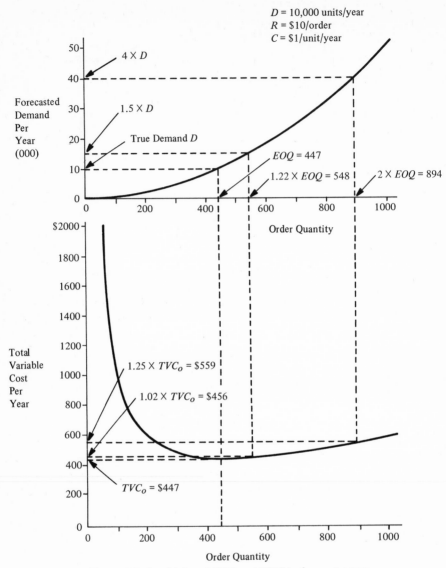

Figure 4-8. Sensitivity of *EOQ* and *TVC* to forecast errors

in the interval .00000 to .16667, the optimal action is to assign one piece of material to each of the four items. In the interval .16667 to .40825, the optimal action is to assign two pieces to the high-valued Item 1 and one each to Items 2 and 3 (or 4).

Now suppose that available evidence narrows the value of *p* to .10 ± .05. Would there be any value in determining the range of *p* more precisely than this? Obviously not, since a more precise estimate would not alter the optimal action and therefore could not add to the expected payoff.

Even if p could exceed .16667, and thus alter the choice of action, the value of greater precision might be quite small. At the critical point of .16667 the optimal action becomes extremely sensitive to the estimate of p. However, the *payoff* tends to be quite *insensitive* to the choice of a "near-optimal" action. For example, if p is in fact .2, the nonoptimal action of assigning one piece of material to each item reduces expected payoffs from 8.16 to 8.00.

Intervals of insensitivity also arise in linear programming models. This can be illustrated by a classic linear programming problem, the assignment of available production capacity to different products. Suppose we have only two types of machine, M_1 and M_2, and two products, P_1 and P_2. Suppose further that we have 16 hours per day of M_1 capacity, and 48 hours per day of M_2 capacity. Each unit of product 1 requires 1 hour on Machine 1 and 6 hours on Machine 2, whereas product 2 requires 2 and 4 hours on Machines 1 and 2, respectively. Assuming that any quantity of either product can be sold at a constant unit profit, the following linear programming problem can be formulated: Maximize

$$z = x_1 p_1 + x_2 p_2$$

subject to

$$1x_1 + 2x_2 \leq 16$$
$$6x_2 + 4x_2 \leq 48$$
$$x_1, x_2 \geq 0$$

where x_i is the quantity produced of product i and p_i is its unit profit.

Figure 4-9 shows the problem in graphical form. The shaded area gives the set of feasible production schedules. Now, suppose that p_1 and p_2 are known. This establishes a family of straight lines having a slope $-p_1/p_2$. Each member of the family has associated with it a unique profit. The farther the line is from the origin, the greater the profit. Therefore, we seek the profit line farthest from the origin that has at least one point included in the feasible region. Any such point is obviously located at one of the vertices of the feasible region (or on a line connecting two vertices), and represents an optimum allocation of capacity.

For example, if $p_1 = p_2 = \$1$ per unit, the optimum schedule is $x_1 = 4$ and $x_2 = 6$. The resulting optimum profit is $4 \cdot 1 + 6 \cdot 1 = 10$. This is shown in Figure 4-10.

If the ratio p_1/p_2 changes, the slope of the profit line changes. However, the optimum point remains the same as long as the ratio is greater

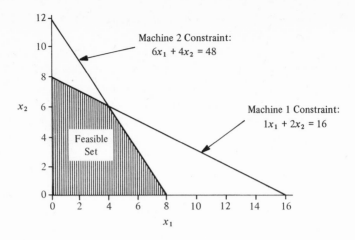

Figure 4-9. Machine scheduling problem

than $\frac{1}{2}$ and less than $\frac{3}{2}$. If the ratio becomes less than $\frac{1}{2}$, the optimum point becomes $x_1 = 0$, $x_2 = 8$. If the ratio exceeds $\frac{3}{2}$, the optimum point switches to $x_1 = 8$, $x_2 = 0$.

Thus, the scheduling decision is completely insensitive to changes in the ratio p_1/p_2 except at the critical values of $\frac{1}{2}$ and $\frac{3}{2}$. Here the decision shifts abruptly with small changes in the ratio. However, even at the critical points *profit* is again fairly insensitive to errors in estimating the values of p_1 and p_2. For example, suppose that p_1 and p_2 are estimated to equal \$2.90 and \$2.00, respectively, so that $p_1/p_2 = 1.45 < \frac{3}{2}$. The optimum schedule would then be calculated to be $x_1 = 4$ and $x_2 = 6$. If, however, p_1 and p_2 turn out to equal \$3.10 and \$2.00, respectively, the true optimum schedule

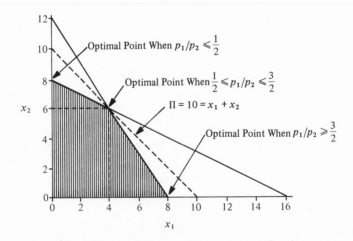

Figure 4-10. Solutions to machine scheduling problem

would be $x_1 = 8$ and $x_2 = 0$ (since $p_1/p_2 = 1.55 > \frac{3}{2}$). The error in estimating the ratio carries the penalty of

$$[(\$3.10) \cdot 8 + (\$2.00) \cdot 0] - [(\$3.10 \cdot 4 + (\$2.00) \cdot 6] = \$24.80 - \$24.40$$
$$= \$0.40$$

Sensitivity Analyses

Any formal model allows some analysis of the sensitivity of payoff to errors in input data. Ideally, one can develop an explicit penalty function having error parameters as independent variables (as in the *EOQ* example). In some cases, sensitivity data can be obtained as a by-product of optimization calculations. At the very least, one can alter input variables to see how such changes affect outcome variables. This can be done whether one is dealing with an analytic or a simulation model. Through a process of selectively varying input data over their estimated range of possible values, the analyst can identify those variables that have little or no effect on outcomes. One can then focus attention on the variables that are revealed to be critical in determining payoff.[22]

If payoff is shown to be highly sensitive to a given variable, effort can be spent on refining the estimate of the variable. In some cases the cost of such refinement might be very great. In others, the inherent statistical variability in a process may simply preclude narrowing the range of an estimate to within the region of relative insensitivity for the variable in question.

Under these circumstances, one should consider the possibility of making structural changes in the physical process being modeled. For example, suppose that costs in a production scheduling model prove to be highly sensitive to forecast accuracy. Rather than try to improve forecasts (which may be subject to only minor improvement), the analyst might better concentrate on structural changes in the production process itself. Such changes might include reducing the lag in processing the sales order, stocking greater component inventory, increasing the flexibility of the manufacturing process to respond to a widely fluctuating product mix, or reducing delivery time through air-freight shipments.

The point is that a sensitivity analysis reveals the critical variables that demand closer attention. In some cases the best approach is to obtain

---

[22] When a model includes a great many input variables, the analyst must be extremely selective in choosing the variables he will vary, since he can explore only a small fraction of the total range of possible input values.

additional information about the sensitive variable; in others, one is advised to live with considerable uncertainty, but to reduce sensitivity through structural changes.

4.5 *Qualitative Evaluation of Value and Cost*

All of the approaches discussed so far require a considerable degree of formalization before one can provide quantitative measures of information value. Increased formalization is taking place at all levels in the organization, but nevertheless it remains true that the potential for quantification is confined to relatively limited areas. When an organization sets out to develop a comprehensive information system, most of the design decisions must be made in the absence of *quantitative* estimates of information value. However, such decisions should at least be guided by certain *qualitative* characteristics of information that govern both its value and cost.

Qualitative Characteristics Determining Value

A given information system can be characterized along several different dimensions. Usually it is not enough merely to list the data elements that are provided as outputs of the system. One must also describe the system in terms of its response time, accuracy, reliability, and similar characteristics. The following discussion focuses on the most important of these characteristics.

Volume of Data.   Since the information system provides an abstract analogue of the organization and its environment, a more detailed analogue gives a higher-resolution representation than does an aggregate analogue. In general, this leads to a higher expected payoff from decisions based on increased detail. This is true so long as the information structure is not already payoff relevant (see page 71). Normally, the system is a long way from exhausting the possibilities for providing useful detail, and therefore increased (relevant) data implies a higher expected payoff.

Just consider some of the potentially useful data that might be included in a corporate data base (*EDP Analyzer,* November 1966). In addition to the present routine files (for example, employee, inventory, stockholders, and so on), a great deal of other data could usefully be added to most existing systems. In the case of a manufacturing process, for instance, operating data might be retained as a means of improving performance predictions (for example, yields and process times), monitoring current operations, and finding ways of improving the process through learning and adaptation. In a retailing operation, retention of past sales data can prove valuable as a means of analyzing the more successful products and identifying the highest potential customers and markets. Whether the increased value of such data justify their cost is an obvious issue, but there can be little doubt that data of this sort add to gross expected payoff.

Increased data handling in functions other than data storage also adds to payoff. Computation, through the use of elaborate models, can increase the accuracy of predicting planning variables. Increased computation allows a more complete search of alternatives and permits the introduction of more variables and greater complexities that enhance the realism of decision-making models. Similarly, increasing data-transmission volumes can lead to better coordination throughout the organization.

Selectivity of Output.   It may be true that a thousand monkeys clattering away on typewriters will eventually produce poetry rivaling Shakespeare's sonnets. However, the effort required to distill out the small dribble of worthwhile poetry from the sea of junk would be immeasurably greater than that required to find another Shakespeare. As much as possible we should avoid requiring a decision maker to scan vast reams of reports in order to select the information he wants. The system itself should do most of the selection and filtering (Ackoff, 1967). By so doing, the system can substantially increase the average surprise content of information displayed and *perceived*. Only after it has been perceived does the information become operational and potentially useful to a human decision maker.

Normally we cannot formalize a situation to the extent that output from the system is so perfectly selective that it identifies only a single optimal action to take. But we can take steps that greatly increase selectivity over that of conventional systems. For example, we can rely much more heavily than at present on *ad hoc* reports rather than broadcasting general-purpose reports that serve everyone and no one. We can also more widely apply the well-known exception principle, in which the system determines by means of control limits when a given type of information should be presented as output. The intent of such methods is to filter out the data that do not significantly alter the decision maker's view of nature.

Selectivity can also be increased by the way in which information is displayed. Good human-factors design can greatly enhance perception. Techniques for increasing perception include the use of standard report formats, graphical displays, and various schemes for drawing attention to the most critical variables (for example, underlining, colors, flashing lights, and so on).

Response Time.[23] Response time can be defined as the time interval required to perform an information-processing operation. The operation in question may involve the updating of a record. In this case response time is the lag between the occurrence of an event and the point at which information about the event is incorporated in the data base. Alternatively, the operation may be the retrieval of data. Here response time is the interval from the initiation of the retrieval until the required response becomes available. Response time of updating and retrieval are thus essentially separate (but obviously related) issues.

Reducing the time to update a record means that the data base provides a more current view of nature. This can be helpful in improving predictions about the future state of planning variables. The prediction span extends from the time the current state of nature was last sensed up to the end of the planning horizon appropriate for a given decision. As shown in Figure 4-11, the prediction span is correspondingly reduced when the lag between

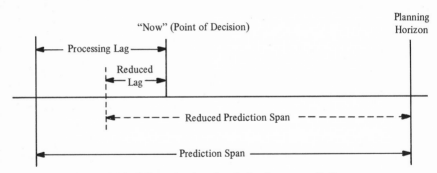

Figure 4-11. Effect of reduced updating lag on prediction span

sensing and decision making is reduced. If the planning horizon extends only a short time into the future, a shorter lag cuts the prediction span significantly. If nature is quite uncertain, any prediction about future states is subject to rapid decay. Under these circumstances, a short prediction span increases accuracy in estimating variables over the planning horizon.[24]

Some decision processes, particularly lower-level operating decisions, require frequent predictions extending only over short horizons. In these cases rapid real-time updating can substantially increase the value of the

[23] See Martin (1967), Chapter 4.

[24] In assessing the value of reduced lag, one must take into account the tradeoff between resources devoted to reducing the lag and those devoted to improving the prediction for a given prediction span. Often the latter approach is to be preferred. For example, a sophisticated sales forecasting model using relatively old data may generate a more accurate prediction than a simple model that has on-line access to "real-time" sales data.

information (Carroll, 1967; *EDP Analyzer,* February 1967). If, on the other hand, the planning horizon is quite long relative to the current lag, reducing the updating lag adds little to predictability. The value of very recent data is therefore small. This tends to be true for higher-level strategic planning.

In some situations information retrieved need not be very recent, but once the information is requested it should be made available quickly. Quick response to queries has particular value under the following circumstances:

1. A decision must be made quickly, and is based on information provided in response to a query formulated at the time the decision is to be made (as in an airline reservation system).
2. A decision is based on information retrieved through sequential queries, in which a given query is formulated on the basis of results obtained from earlier queries. This kind of serial probing tends to be very useful in making complex, unstructured decisions of the type facing strategic planners.
3. A problem is sufficiently complex that the decision maker requires significant "make-ready" time to familiarize himself with the current status of the problem. A quick response—in the order of perhaps a few seconds—allows him to retain a more complete grasp of the problem. Although the issue is not without controversy, there seems to be good evidence that quick-response man–machine systems can substantially amplify the effectiveness of human decision making. Computer programming and certain engineering design problems provide the best current examples of this (Grant and Sackman, 1967).

Accuracy and Reliability. In the case of decision processes that deal with unaggregated data, the value of information may be highly sensitive to errors. For example, an error in a bank account balance may be very expensive indeed. When data are aggregated for high-level decision making, such as an analysis of bank deposits by state, the value of great accuracy drops off sharply.

Accuracy refers not only to the degree to which sensed information corresponds to the entity it purports to measure; it also applies to the degree to which a *predicted* value (such as a sales forecast) corresponds to the eventual actual value. The latter depends on the way in which sensed data are transformed into predictions.

If the values over time of a given variable exhibit some stability (for example, if the current rate of sales is related to previous rates), random errors in sensing or prediction can be reduced by "smoothing" the data through an averaging process. Increasing the time span over which data are averaged reduces the random component of the resulting average at the expense of reducing its recency (Forrester, 1961, pp. 406–411). For example, a daily sales rate averaged over a six-day week will be subject to less random variation than the rates over the individual days, but the average age of the data will be six times as great (three days versus half a day). Thus a tradeoff often exists between accuracy and recency.

A reliable system is one that functions satisfactorily with a high probability. Such a system reduces the cost penalties sustained when a breakdown occurs. It also permits the organization to get by with a less costly back-up system capable of taking over in the event of a failure of the main system.

Generality and Flexibility.   A general system is one that can meet a wide variety of output requirements without any basic modifications. A flexible system is one that can be modified relatively easily.

Both generality and flexibility increase the system's ability to provide outputs that were not fully anticipated at the time the system was installed. In a shifting environment, and as information accumulates about the environment and decision processes, output needs can never be completely predicted. Changes will take place; the only question at issue is the responsiveness of the system in adapting to current needs.

A specialized, inflexible system is always out of step with recognized needs for information. Decisions made in the absence of such information will tend, therefore, to yield a lower payoff than they would otherwise.

Cost of Information

Not a great deal need be said about the cost of information. Determining the cost of a given information structure is a relatively straightforward—albeit formidable—exercise. It entails a translation of desired information outputs into a system capable of providing them. The desired output characteristics imply certain storage and processing capacities, data collection and transmission volumes, and trained manpower for implementing and operating the system. The cost of the total system is the sum of all these resources.[25]

---

[25] As in all cost analyses, the actual determination of cost involves some exceedingly difficult conceptual problems. This is especially true of computer systems, since they exhibit such a high proportion of fixed and joint costs that cannot be assigned to individual data elements except through essentially arbitrary allocation.

The cost of a specific system is thus largely a technical matter. But two systems may provide identical outputs while costing substantially different amounts because of differences in their efficiency. In the discussion that follows we shall assume that alternative systems can be implemented with equal efficiency. We thereby limit discussion to costs that are variable only with respect to the characteristics of information outputs.

Cost is also dependent on the state of information technology. As technology advances, a given set of outputs can be obtained for lower cost (or, alternatively, improved information can be had for the same cost). When this occurs, the optimal balance between value and cost tends to shift toward improved information quality.

All too often, "cost" tends to mean one that shows up in the current budget of the data processing department. A consideration of the full costs of information must include the costs incurred by the user in converting the output from the formal system into a more usable form. These might include, for example, the cost of manually scanning bulky reports to extract shreds of useful information. Total costs also include the resources required to maintain the system and keep it responsive to current needs—costs that are incurred long after the original system has been implemented and debugged.

In the very short run, all costs tend to be largely fixed. Short-run changes in outputs may or may not be possible, but costs will remain much the same in either case. Since only variable costs are relevant in assessing the cost of information, short-run costs tend to be very low. For example, if the computer is idle during part of the day, only a small incremental cost may be incurred in using it to generate information not otherwise available.[26] In the long run, however, virtually all costs are variable and therefore relevant in assessing the cost of a change in the output from the system. Most major changes in a system involve an implementation lag sufficiently long that costs can be considered largely variable. Subsequent discussion will primarily concern long-run cost behavior.

Costs thus defined are related to the same qualitative characteristics that govern value. Not surprisingly, characteristics that add to a system's gross value also add to its cost.

Volume of data.   The amount of data handled by a system has a strong effect on its cost. Costs tend not to increase in proportion to volume, however. Substantial economies of scale exist in performing certain data pro-

---

[26] This is not true, of course, if an external market exists for excess computer time.

cessing functions. This is particularly true in the case of computation and data transmission (see page 60).

As volume grows, the point may be reached at which costs start to climb steeply. This is certainly true in the short run, where capacity constraints are significant. Even in the long run, certain problems tend to grow disproportionately as volume increases. For example, the administrative overhead required to implement and manage a system may become burdensome as it grows in complexity. The cost of retrieving specific data also may rise more than linearly as the size of the data base grows.

Selectivity of Output.   Increasing selectivity affects costs in several ways. A periodic, general-purpose report can be produced relatively cheaply compared with providing each user with a tailor-made response to his *ad hoc* requests for information. A special-purpose report must be described in some language and then processed, perhaps by itself. Producing such reports tends to be expensive.

Exception reporting, another way of increasing selectivity, involves extra systems design and information processing. Ideally, an exception is reported only when an unplanned action must be taken in response to errors in the existing plan. But the need for a change arises when the current plan is not deemed to be the optimal one in light of new information. Therefore, identification of a real exception implies knowledge of the optimal plan. Since such knowledge is not generally available to the systems, we must settle for considerably less than perfect exception reporting.

Errors in reporting take the form of (1) failure to identify true exceptions, and (2) incorrectly tagging as an exception that which does not require a change in plan. The former is usually felt to be the more serious error, and so the normal bias is to report situations that give any evidence of requiring attention. It is then up to the human decision maker to apply more sophisticated filters to isolate the few really critical exceptions. In an effort to increase selectivity, one must pay an increasingly high cost in added systems complexity to reduce the probability of reporting errors.

Response Time.   Cost as a function of response time depends heavily on the way in which transactions are processed. The transactions may be entered to update the data base, or they may be inquiry transactions. In either case, if a relatively long response time is permitted, sequential processing is clearly the more efficient means. For one thing, sequential processing allows the use of inexpensive off-line storage (such as magnetic tape), since only a selected portion of the data base is accessed during any one processing run. Sequential processing can also provide, in the case of high-activity files, a very low average access time to records.

In order to reduce the response time with sequential processing, the interval between successive batches must be reduced. In many cases, a fairly high proportion of processing cost is accounted for by the fixed time required to read and write the master file. Therefore, cost per transaction tends to be inversely proportional to processing interval (and hence to response time).

As the desired response time is reduced, eventually the point is reached at which random processing becomes cheaper than sequential processing. Random processing is fairly expensive per transaction, since it requires on-line storage and involves relatively long access times to obtain desired records. On the other hand, the cost of random processing tends to be quite insensitive to changes in response time. This is so because each transaction is handled essentially independently, and thus little saving is realized by accumulating a number of transactions over a batch cycle and processing them together.[27]

With random processing, each transaction is handled .as a batch of one item, and so no batching delay is introduced. Random response thus consists of three components: (1) actual processing time, which tends to be very short; (2) accesses to the on-line files, which may be significant, particularly if a series of accesses is required; and (3) the time the transaction is sitting in a queue waiting for input, output, storage, or processing resources, which often is the largest single component of lag. A reduction in response time is effected primarily through increasing slack capacity of the system, thus reducing queue time. This, of course, adds to cost.

Response time can be reduced through means other than computation time. Data transmission is particularly susceptible to a drastic time reduction. A premium is paid for electrical transmission compared to the cost of physically transporting the stored medium. The time span to transmit a given message depends on the channel capacity of the transmission circuit and the relation of capacity to the average load. Response time can be reduced, at a cost, by increasing capacity.

Accuracy and Reliability.   Almost any degree of perfection can be achieved, but cost tends to rise very steeply as perfection is approached.

---

[27] When the transaction rate is high enough that several transactions may occur during an allowed response time, it may be economical to process transactions sequentially from a direct-access storage medium such as disk. The batch cycle in this case may be as short as a fraction of a minute.

Accuracy is achieved primarily through redundancy. Duplication, check digits, reasonableness checks, validity checks—all of these error-control techniques rely ultimately on some form of redundancy, and all cost money in the form of extra data collection, transmission, storage, or processing.

Reliability is a matter of both hardware and software (Martin, 1967, Chapter 6). Hardware reliability can be achieved through conservative design, frequent diagnostic checking, and equipment redundancy, all of which entail some cost. Software reliability stems from following such good design techniques as straightforward programming, modularity, and careful systems testing. Again, some price must be paid for any increase in reliability.

Generality.   Generality adds to the cost of designing and implementing a system, since it is achieved by including a variety of features in the system. Other costs are also incurred. As variety goes up, so does the problem of specifying which of the alternative options to exercise in a specific case. For example, if an inventory control system allows several ways of calculating order points, then someone must specify which method to use for a given item. This adds to the costs of training personnel to use the system.

Furthermore, a general system tends to be somewhat inefficient in the use of computer resources. The program is larger and therefore demands more storage space. It is inevitably slower than a special-purpose program, since it is encumbered by the requirement to perform logical tests to determine the specific conditions that apply in a particular case. It is also denied possibilities for exploiting special circumstances that permit shortcuts.

There is another side to the picture, however. Increased generality may actually lower the cost *per application* by permitting wider use of a program. Furthermore, good programming technique can achieve considerable generality at negligible cost—for example, by eliminating most constants from a program and treating them instead as parameters to be read in at execution time. Training costs can be reduced by designing the system to select automatically a standard default option in the absence of specific instructions to the contrary. Finally, the price of lower machine efficiency due to generality is becoming less significant as the cost of computation goes down.

Flexibility.   Flexibility is achieved primarily through good design practice. Simple, straightforward programs are much more easily modified than tricky ones that strive for the last measure of machine efficiency. A program written in a higher-level language is likewise more flexible than one written in a machine language. Thorough documentation is essential if programs are to be modified after the original programmer has forgotten its details or left the organization.

Flexibility is also increased tremendously when the system is designed in modular fashion. Such a system is composed of relatively independent modules or subroutines, and the bulk of communications among modules takes place in the form of explicitly defined parameters. A change in one part of the system can affect other parts only through the parameters. All other changes are strictly internal to a module, and therefore subtle effects of a change cannot be transmitted to other parts of the system.

The techniques for achieving flexibility generally carry some price in extra design and programming effort and reduced machine efficiency. These costs tend to be trivial, however, compared to the less obvious ones stemming from inflexible designs.

Balancing Value and Cost

Placing a value on information can best be done by users of the information. Determination of cost, on the other hand, is the responsibility of systems specialists. A properly designed system must balance the cost and value of information, but in most cases the user and the specialist do not understand each other's jobs sufficiently well for either party to strike a suitable balance on his own.

The specification of the output from a system is ultimately the responsibility of the users. In order to perform this role, however, the specialists must identify the tradeoffs available. For example, if a manager asks for a maximum response time of ten seconds, he should at least be made aware that an increase to 30 seconds would save, say, $10,000 a year. He may insist on the shorter time, but at least he has been afforded the opportunity to reach a subjective balance between value and cost. Without such feedback from the specialist, the user is forced to make choices without knowing their consequences. An essential part of any successful systems-design effort is, therefore, a constant dialogue between user and design specialist.

CHAPTER 5

Planning and Control

5.1 *The Role of Plans*

Planning has been given a variety of meanings. In its broadest sense, it is "deciding in advance what is to be done" (Newman, 1951, p. 15). Defined in such sweeping terms, planning necessarily precedes all action, if only in the mind of the person performing the action. Any attempt to make significant improvements in the process must deal primarily with relatively *formal* planning that involves the explicit evaluation of alternative courses of action, selection of one of the alternatives for execution, and formal communication of the decision to interested persons throughout the organization.

A great many different types of activity fall within such a definition. Among them are the design of the organizational structure and goals, selection of resources, specification of policies and procedures, budgeting, systems design, product design, and detailed scheduling (Goetz, 1949, p. 2). All of these varied activities together comprise the planning network by which the organization governs itself.

A *plan* constitutes the output from any planning process. Thus, organizational goals, policies, strategies, budgets, procedures, rules, programs, and schedules represent various forms of plans (Koontz and O'Donnell, 1964, pp. 74–78). The purpose of a plan is to bring about behavior that leads to desired outcomes. In order to do this, a formal plan must (1) describe actions and outcomes and (2) serve as a formal vehicle of coordination.

The Plan As a Description of Actions and Outcomes

Planning provides the primary source of coordination within the organization, and plans represent the "messages" by which the system communicates among organizational units. The form of communication may vary. A plan may continue in effect until explicitly rescinded or modified, to be evoked under specified conditions or by a higher-level plan. Goals, policies, procedures, and "standing plans" (Newman, 1951, p. 18) have this characteristic. They represent continuing *performance programs* (March and Simon, 1958, pp. 141–150) by which higher levels in the organization govern lower-level behavior. They permit the organization to deal economically with routine, high-volume activities that otherwise might swamp decision channels[1] (Morris, 1968, pp. 54–56).

On the other hand, *ad hoc* plans may be devised to describe behavior over a specified planning horizon. Project plans and periodic budgets and schedules are examples of these "single-use" plans.

Occasionally, it may be necessary to formulate two or more alternative "contingency" plans, deferring the choice of the specific alternative to execute until additional information is available (such as the strategy followed by a competitor or opponent). However, the added cost of generating multiple *ad hoc* plans is justified only in those cases in which plans cannot otherwise be formulated and disseminated within the required response time.

Sometimes it is advantageous to express a plan in a functional form in which the values of certain variables are initially left unspecified. For instance, a "variable" budget might define a resource input (such as cost) as a function of output (such as production quantity). Once the functional relationship is established, the determination of a specific plan involves merely the evaluation of the function when the values of the unspecified variables become known. This scheme offers the double advantage of

---

[1] Standardized procedures do, however, carry the risk of treating nonroutine events in a routine fashion. The difficulty arises in classifying an event as "routine" (in which case standard procedures apply) or as "nonroutine" (which calls for special treatment). Bureaucratic systems are not noted for dealing wisely with this issue.

drastically reducing planning response time and lowering the cost of repetitive planning. The functional relationship need not be formulated again until a significant change occurs in the underlying conditions on which it is based.

A plan may be quite specific, leaving very little discretion to those responsible for its execution. It may, on the other hand, merely provide loose guidelines, such as an overall return-on-investment goal. It may also prohibit or require only certain actions, as in the case of a policy that requires the purchasing department to maintain alternative sources of supply.

Plans, like computer programs, may be expressed in either *procedural* or *declarative* form.[2] A procedural plan specifies a step-by-step sequence of actions that presumably will lead to a known (and desired) outcome. Alternatively, a declarative plan specifies only a desired outcome, and leaves to those executing it the responsibility for choosing the sequence of actions necessary to achieve it. Often, the same plan has both procedural and declarative aspects.

Some plans are expressed in narrative form, such as a description of a personnel policy. More commonly, however, a plan is expressed in terms of quantitative variables. A manufacturing plan, for example, is described in terms of units of production, manpower levels, costs, and the like. The variables provide only an abstract representation of planned behavior. This is particularly true of high-level plans dealing largely with gross aggregates. But even in its most detailed form, a plan specifies an extremely sparse set of variables out of the infinite set possible.

The specification of a given quantitative plan consists of placing values on its variables or establishing its functional form. Independence obviously does not exist among all of the variables and relationships that could be used to describe a plan. The choice of the decisions that are treated as independent is essentially arbitrary, and depends to a considerable extent on computational efficiency and on how the planner[3] chooses to express his decisions. Those decisions used for this purpose will be called *decision* variables. All other variables used to describe a plan will be termed *outcome* variables. The value of an outcome variable is implied by the choice of the decision variables.

[2] Procedural and declarative descriptions correspond, respectively, to process and state descriptions (Simon, 1962, p. 479) or to activity and product specifications (March and Simon, 1958, pp. 144–146).

[3] I use the term *planner* to describe the person having decision-making authority for planning at a given level in the organization. The planner may, of course, be assisted by a staff, and in practice it may be difficult to pinpoint the real locus of decision making because of a certain amount of diffusion of effective authority.

These notions can be illustrated by an inventory control example. A given inventory plan may be described by such variables as the aggregate inventory investment, the planned stockout probability, and the imputed interest rate on funds invested in inventory. Once an algorithm has been specified for determining inventory decisions (constituting a higher-level plan), the stockout probability and imputed interest rate can be treated as decision variables. The resulting aggregate inventory investment represents an outcome variable. If, on the other hand, an algorithm exists for allocating aggregate inventory among individual items (see, for example, Emery, 1960), then aggregate inventory can be treated as a decision variable and stockout probability as an outcome variable.

In choosing a plan, the planner naturally tries to use a set of decision variables that will lead to satisfactory organizational behavior. The variables ignored are assumed to be irrelevant, insignificant, or implied by the accomplishment of the decision variables. (Significant variables may be simply overlooked, of course.) For example, meeting a production schedule defined in terms of units completed may imply satisfactory performance in terms of stability of employment, delivery performance, and inventory level. The decision variables must close "loopholes" sufficiently well that achievement of the defined plan will in fact have desirable consequences. Ordinarily, this requires the specification of time-phased plans in physical units, cost units, and units that measure capital investment (Goetz, 1949, pp. 92–115).

The planner must guard against treating as a decision variable that which is implied by the choice of other variables. For instance, the planner in the previous illustration cannot simultaneously specify aggregate inventory and stockout probability. Unless he just happens to choose consistent values, such a plan would prove infeasible. Under these circumstances, something must give: either the plan as described by the decision variables will not be achieved, or it will be achieved at the expense of some other variables (inventory reordering cost, say). Unfortunately, the complexity of organizational planning often makes it extremely difficult to determine the extent to which the value of one variable is implied by the choice of others.

Outcome variables provide a means of characterizing the consequences stemming from a given choice of decision variables. The planner may be interested in a vast number of different outcome variables, each of them furnishing a different view of the same underlying plan. A five-year corporate budget, for example, might be described by such outcome variables as profit, return on investment, sales, production, and the ending balance of current assets for each of the years included in the total budgeting span. One outcome variable may be a function of other outcome variables—an aggregation of different cost classifications, say, or the discounted present value of similar costs incurred in different time periods.

If the planner does not know the relationship existing between two outcome variables, he might wish to describe a plan in terms of both, even though one is clearly subsumed under the other. For example, profit and the inventory stockout rate of finished goods might both be used as outcome variables, although presumably the latter is of no inherent interest except insofar as it has some (generally unknown) effect on long-range profit.

If it is feasible to do so, the description of a plan should recognize the fact that most outcome variables cannot be predicted with certainty. An outcome might, for example, be defined in terms of a confidence interval or probability distribution, rather than by a single value. Unfortunately, the determination of such probabilistic outcome variables can add enormously to the cost of planning and control. Often it is necessary to treat the world as though it were deterministic, leaving to the planner the task of compensating for uncertainty. (He can be aided in this, however, by a sensitivity analysis that determines the effect on the outcome variables of changes in underlying random variables. See Section 4.4.)

A decision variable such as aggregate inventory may have intrinsic interest in its own right, as well as serving as a description of controllable behavior. The complete description of an alternative plan should include, therefore, both decision and outcome variables. In most cases, of course, the simultaneous display of all relevant variables would be awkward and confusing. The important factor is not what *is* displayed, but what potentially *can be* displayed. Ideally, the planner should be able to call for a selective display of those variables in which he is currently interested.[4]

The issue involved in choosing decision and outcome variables as a description of alternative plans is precisely the same as choosing variables for management reports that measure past events. The only difference between the two is that planning deals with anticipated consequences, whereas the typical management report deals with actual consequences (insofar as they are correctly sensed and reported). In both cases the objective is to

---

[4] Conceptually, it is often useful to think of a network of plans described in matrix form. Goetz (1965), for example, uses such a format, in which cost and revenue classifications are listed in one dimension and time periods in the other. The programming system for the Office of the Secretary of Defense (1962, pp. II-5–II-9) uses a similar conceptual display of plans, in which physical or dollar resource inputs represent one dimension of the array and outputs (expressed in terms of *program elements,* or units of military force such as Minuteman squadrons) represent the other dimension.

capture the essence of a situation with relatively few variables. In order to achieve this, the system should increase selectivity of the information displayed by permitting *ad hoc* inquiries and by performing exception reporting (which, in the case of planning, would reveal aspects of an alternative plan that are exceptionally good or bad compared to other alternatives).

The Plan As a Formal Vehicle of Coordination

A plan not only describes desired behavior, but it also serves as a formal vehicle for communication throughout the organization. With this philosophy, the act of choosing a plan (or, equivalently, approving one proposed by a lower-level unit) constitutes one of the most important functions of management.

Plans in their various forms provide the basic source of information for predicting the actions of others. This is true of both standing and single-use plans. Standing plans—in the broadest sense, policies, procedures, and all other types of programmed activity—play much the same role as habit in biological organisms. They provide organizational stability, and thus increase the accuracy with which one unit can predict the behavior of another. This allows a unit to formulate its own plan on the basis of an assumed or provisional level of activity in other parts of the organization. Single-use plans describe explicitly the anticipated activity of the units included in the plans. They are transmitted to appropriate planners throughout the organization as a basis for their own planning.

Upon approval, a plan becomes part of a network of plans that serves as the basis for execution and coordination. Any significant addition, deletion, or modification of a specific plan should be effected only through the same official approval mechanism that first authorized it. Failure to do this may rob the plan of its integrity and thwart the objectives of the original planner.

In order for the approved plan network to play this central role, it must be based on the best current predictions of future events (within allowed error tolerances). This, in turn, calls for a control system that senses actual events and compares them with the predictions on which the current plans are based. If a significant deviation occurs, the control system should signal the need for new planning that takes into account the most recent available feedback information about the environment. With such a control system to "close the loop," planners at all levels in the organization can look to the latest plan network as a reliable source of information for execution and further planning.

Management under these circumstances can largely focus on the planning process. Far from being just a sterile paperwork or bureaucratic activity, planning should provide the basic means of directing the behavior of the organization. It is not exaggerating too much to view a high-level manager as a planner who lives largely in an analogue, abstract world involving the predicted future. He is affected by the real world only to the extent that feedback information is available to modify planning data. The planner, like the brain (Bishop, 1960), is forever cut off from the world "out there," and can perceive things only through highly filtered information channels.

Gardner (1964, pp. 78–79) points out the dangers of placing too heavy a reliance on formal information systems. Raw data are "sampled, screened, condensed, compiled, coded, expressed in statistical form, spun into generalizations and crystallized into recommendations" before reaching high-level planners. In the process, "emotions, feeling, sentiment, mood and almost all the irrational nuances of human situations" are filtered out, and therefore the information cannot convey what is really going on in the world.

The danger certainly exists that a high-level planner will not be provided relevant information about the world. But the real world is a very complicated place, and a high-level planner inevitably perceives it in an exceedingly abstracted form. This is true whether he obtains the information through firsthand observation or through a formal information system. Such a planner faces a world of vast scope, and therefore he *must* rely primarily on a formal information system to filter out "noise" and less important data and to provide an abstraction of the real world that preserves essential information about significant events. From the standpoint of information gathering, visits by the planner to the "front lines" can only furnish a small sample with which he can verify and add realism to information provided by the formal information system. (But personal contact with lower levels in the organization serve other purposes besides information gathering, of course.)

5.2 *Planning Goals*[5]

The goals assigned a planner play an important part in governing his choice among his available alternatives. It will be useful, therefore, to examine the nature of these goals and their effect on behavior.

[5] Simon (1964) contributes his usual wisdom to this topic.

Generation of Multidimensional Goals

The goals assigned to a planner are normally multidimensional. There are three principal reasons for this. In the first place, compression of several incommensurable goals into a single one reduces their information content. Unless there exists a general consensus about the tradeoff between goals— one that is acceptable for purposes of all lower-level planning and control —then an arbitrary tradeoff function suppresses information that lower-level planners should have in formulating their own plans. The incommensurable goals facing a high-level planner must, therefore, normally be passed down to lower-level planners in some translated multidimensional form. The incommensurable global objectives—dealing with profit, esthetics, and morality, say—thus tend to trickle down through the goal hierarchy.

Suppose, for example, that a plant superintendent is assigned the goals of reducing costs and preventing accidents. He naturally wants to assign goals to foremen that will lead to the accomplishment of his own goals. Conceivably, he could collapse his two goals into a single-dimensional cost goal by assessing a penalty cost for any accidents that occur in a foreman's department. However, it is extremely unlikely that a generally agreed value could (or would) be placed on each type of accident.

For one thing, the superintendent would, no doubt, be loathe to expose himself to criticism by making an explicit tradeoff between cost and safety (although he makes an implicit tradeoff every time he allocates resources for safety purposes). Furthermore, in most cases he lacks knowledge of the implications of a particular tradeoff decision, and would therefore not want to turn over to a foreman the authority to take an unsafe action simply because it is judged by the foreman to be consistent with a cost goal.

Multiple goals are also created as an approximation for a single "real" goal that cannot be measured in practice. Business profit is a case in point. The determination of real profit as the economist defines it requires the calculation of the present value of the firm at the beginning and end of the period over which profit is being measured (Alexander, 1962). This, in turn, requires a knowledge of future cash flows (and a suitable discount rate). Such a goal therefore provides little operational guidance for making planning decisions.

Accounting "profit," on the other hand, provides a useful and measurable approximation to real profit through a process of matching the revenues and costs associated with a given period's activity. This matching typically requires a great many essentially arbitrary allocations of costs and revenues among different accounting classifications and time periods. Nevertheless, the conventions used for this purpose offer reasonably well-defined and operational procedures for calculating "profit."

Profit defined by accounting conventions depends primarily on *past* costs, and therefore may be inconsistent with *future* profits. In recognition of this fact, managers are typically held accountable for subsidiary goals other than just accounting profit. For instance, each planner may be assigned certain "position" or "ending status" goals—Likert (1961, pp. 61–62) uses the term *intervening variables*—expressed in terms of such variables as market participation, product-development expenditures, cost-reduction targets, and employee turnover.

These multiple goals are designed to make the planner concern himself with longer-range profits as well as the immediate profit. By means of such goals, planners receive early readings on the status of the organization in order that they need not wait until the distant future reveals the effects of current decisions.[6] Subsidiary goals thus provide a feedback loop having a much shorter time delay than an "end result" goal such as profit (Ashby, 1956, pp. 221–225).

Finally, multiple goals are often generated as a means of coping with interactions. It is often not possible to devise a single goal that embodies all of the relevant factors and interacting effects that a lower-level planner should consider in selecting a plan among the alternatives available. It may be necessary, therefore, to use multiple goals in order to convey sufficient information about desired behavior in the face of interactions (Whinston, 1962, pp. VI 33–44).

Suppose, for example, that the president of a company wishes to assign goals to the vice-president of manufacturing that will lead to a satisfactory accounting profit. Certainly a single-dimension profit goal cannot be used, since he shares this responsibility with other departments.[7] Even though the manufacturing department may be primarily concerned with costs, it also affects sales revenue through such means as product quality and stock

---

[6] Position variables used as organizational goals serve the same purpose as they do in other types of problem-solving situation. For example, in the game of checkers or chess, the astronomical number of alternatives precludes an exhaustive tracing of every chain of moves to the completion of the game. Instead, the player (or a heuristic computer program) traces a selected chain of moves a relatively short number of moves ahead. He must then assess each resulting end position in order to evaluate the sequence of moves that led to it (Samuel, 1959).

[7] Manufacturing "profit" can be computed by use of transfer prices, but in most cases such a figure is essentially arbitrary. Under some circumstances, however, "shadow" prices that reflect current marginal costs can be used as a tool of resource allocation among interacting activities (Arrow, 1959).

availability. Therefore, the vice-president should not be held responsible only for costs; he should also meet quality and delivery goals (among others).

The Behavior Induced by Assigned Goals[8]

The organization must assume that each planner will take his goals seriously by attempting to "optimize" in terms of the goals assigned him. This is true whether or not the resulting behavior in fact contributes to the success of the organization as a whole. Thus, if a sales manager is held responsible solely for sales volume, he may strive for increased dollar sales even at the expense of reduced corporate profit (by granting too many price concessions to customers, for example). A planner, like a magic genie, is apt to interpret his goals literally; therefore, the organization should expect to get exactly what it asks for.

We must, of course, distinguish between *formal* and *effective* goals. The organization may adopt a set of stated goals, which may or may not be the effective ones. The real goals are those that receive emphasis in the complex reward-and-punishment structure of the organization. A plant superintendent may profess interest in good housekeeping, but if he bases all promotions and Christmas bonuses only on manufacturing costs, then he should not be too surprised if a foreman pays scant attention to the tidiness of his department. Similarly, if a president punishes his vice-presidents for their every failure, then he will breed extreme conservatism within the firm despite any amount of exhortation or formal goals that attempt to foster initiative and willingness to take justified risks.

The choice of goals that lead to desirable behavior is by no means a simple matter. For most purposes it is necessary to express goals in an operational form that permits quantification of plans and measurement of results (Haberstroh, 1958, pp. 69–70). Nonquantitative goals are, of course, also employed; but quantified goals tend to drive out, in Gresham-like fashion, all other goals. Thus, college deans may find it easier to justify faculty promotions based on the number of research publications than on the quality of teaching.

A goal may not always be amenable to quantification. "High employee morale" and "effective research" may be laudable goals, but they are difficult to measure. In such cases, the organization must resort to the use of goal substitutes, or *surrogates,* that presumably approximate the real goals

---

[8] Issues involved in setting goals are discussed in detail by Hughes (1965).

(in the sense that the surrogates induce behavior consistent with the real goals). For example, morale may be gauged by the amount of absenteeism, and research effectiveness may be measured by the number of patent disclosures.

The use of measurable goal surrogates is essential, but it also carries some obvious hazards. The variables employed may not, in fact, be closely correlated with real goals, and therefore the resulting behavior need not be desirable in terms of real goals. For example, a foreman may be induced to browbeat employees if they legitimately take time off, and the research director may be induced to work on trivial projects offering as their sole merit a high probability of yielding patent disclosures. Distortions of this sort cannot be avoided altogether, but a judicious selection of goal variables can mitigate their undesirable effects.

As a partial solution to this problem, a planner can be assigned goals having upper and lower limits. The lower limit might represent performance considered attainable with a high probability. It can serve, therefore, as a standard of minimum acceptable performance and as a basis for all other planning throughout the organization. A cash budget, for example, could be developed on the assumption that all units will at least meet their minimum profit goal.

The upper limit under this scheme provides a standard of superior performance—a goal the planner must stretch to reach. Performance "better" than the upper limit would not be encouraged, since the planner might otherwise be induced to devote an undue amount of resources and effort to one goal at the expense of his other goals (Schleh, 1961, pp. 32–36). Thus, an upper limit on manufacturing quality would encourage the foreman to strive for "high," but not "excessive," quality.

5.3 *The Hierarchical Nature of Planning*

Planning Levels

Planning is designed to achieve behavior consistent with the overall global goals of the organization. But global goals become operational only after they have been factored into a hierarchy of subgoals. The factoring is accomplished through planning. Each subgoal generated by this process gives rise to lower-level planning, which, in turn, may generate still lower-level subgoals as a means of achieving its own goals.[9]

[9] See Section 1.3. Hierarchical control is also discussed by Powers, Clark, and McFarland (1960); Mesarovic (1962); Williamson (1967); and Williams (1968).

It is the responsibility of a planner to perform the translation of his plan into lower-level plans in a way that maintains consistency between levels. If this is done, the complete set of plans throughout the organization constitutes a hierarchical description of intended behavior. Plans at all levels describe portions of the same total behavior, but the precision of the description increases as high-level plans are amplified into lower-level plans.

In the process of elaborating higher-level plans, each level in the planning hierarchy adds information to the description of intended behavior. Eventually the network (hopefully) describes desired behavior unambiguously enough to achieve the planned outcomes within reasonable limits. Even at the lowest planning level, however, plans normally do not spell out every detail. Conceptually, one should continue the hierarchical planning process until the cost of additional formal planning exceeds the expected marginal improvement that it brings.[10]

The hierarchical nature of planning is manifested in three primary ways: (1) scope of planning, (2) degree of aggregation of planning variables, and (3) the time sequence in which the planning occurs.

High-level planning concerns itself with issues having broad scope in terms of organizational activity and time. This is necessary in order to more closely approximate the global goals of the organization. Thus, a high-level "strategic" plan may describe behavior for the entire organization or major portions of it, and the planning horizon may extend far into the future. Low-level plans, on the other hand, pertain to very limited activities and extend over a relatively short horizon.

High-level planning uses very aggregate variables, while lower-level planning deals with detailed, disaggregated data. Because of the economic and technical limitations on information handling, higher-level planning must sacrifice detail to gain scope. It does this by aggregating data over such dimensions as time, products, organizational units, and functions. (In order to combine dissimilar items, the aggregation is generally weighted by monetary value or some other measure of resource content such as labor hours.) For example, a corporate financial plan might use annual time increments, dollar values of broad product classes, and highly aggregated cost classifications. A low-level plan, such as a production schedule, might deal with hourly time increments, specific products or components, and specific physical resources.

All planning is directed toward some set of assigned goals. It is also subject to constraints imposed by the existing organizational structure, limi-

---

[10] Some plans are expressed in great detail. For example, in the case of certain highly repetitive manual tasks, the planning hierarchy might terminate at the very detailed micromotion or "therblig" level.

tations on physical resources and available information, and procedures of various kinds. All of these factors that impinge on lower-level planning are the product of earlier planning decisions (and the effect of external factors).

Consider the effect of a resource constraint set by higher-level planning. Lower-level planning must recognize the availability of such resources as capital equipment, managerial talent, manpower, material, and energy. Instead of "congealed" physical resources, a planner may be granted a flexible resource in the form of an aggregate money constraint (which, of course, congeals upon use). The current amount of each available resource is presumably reflected in the planning data used in lower-level planning.

Information constitutes the raw material for planning. Higher-level plans partially govern lower-level planning by means of the information they make available. For example, the organization employs uncertainty absorption as a way of achieving some direction and consistency over lower-level planning (see page 43). Transfer prices provide another means for guiding lower-level planning.

Technical knowledge represents a special kind of information. Although the fund of technical knowledge is by no means completely controllable by the organization, it is certainly subject to some control through the organization's allocation of resources to research and development activities.

Performance programs of one form or another are used by the organization to govern lower-level planning. Constraints on planning can be imposed through a hierarchy of standing plans, standard operating procedures, policies, and computational algorithms (March and Simon, 1958, pp. 141–150).

The specific way in which a constraint impinges on planning often depends on the procedures used by lower-level processes. A given constraint may be considered either as a goal or as a parameter of a procedure. For example, an aggregate inventory level set by a high-level planner may be treated as a parameter in a procedure for allocating inventory subject to an aggregate constraint. Alternatively, if the inventory level cannot be handled conveniently as a parameter, it becomes a goal that the lower-level planner considers in selecting alternative plans.

Centralization Versus Decentralization

Goals and constraints restrict the range of acceptable plans generated by a lower-level planner. That, in fact, is their purpose: to constrain—perhaps "guide" or "motivate" would be a less negatively loaded term—lower-level planning in a way that better ensures that plans throughout the organization conform to the organization's global goals. For example, the basic (but rather ill-defined) objectives of the organization provide a guide for the generation of its "long-range" plan that, in turn, constrains the preparation of its annual budget. The constraints imposed by higher-level planning may be loose and subject to revision, but it is difficult to see the purpose they serve unless they play a definite role in the generation of lower-level plans.

Goals and constraints restrict the range of alternatives in different ways. Goals establish criteria by which a planner can assess the relative merit of alternatives open to him by virtue of his available physical resources. Sometimes goals are expressed as thresholds or constraints on allowed action. The distinction is largely arbitrary; both should be viewed as a means of guiding the choice among alternatives (Simon, 1964, pp. 3–6). Constraints on available resources and information, however, operate somewhat differently: they make it physically impossible or very costly for the lower-level planner to follow certain courses of action.

The number of alternative plans consistent with a planner's goals and constraints provides a useful conceptual measure of centralization: If the high-level plan imposes severe constraints that allow relatively few options, then that stage of the planning hierarchy can be viewed as being relatively centralized. If the high-level plan leaves a great many options, the process at that stage is decentralized (Emery, 1964). Planning can, of course, be relatively decentralized at one level and centralized at another.

Because centralization restricts lower-level actions, it should be justified only on the grounds that the restrictions lead to better overall behavior of the organization. This is true only when significant interactions exist between lower-level units. If a subunit interacts very weakly with other parts of the organization, it is desirable to assign the subunit only loose goals consistent with those of the organization as a whole (a "suitable" return on investment, say). In this way, the subunit is free to exploit its own detailed knowledge of its operations and environment.

If significant interactions exit, on the other hand, loose goals do not provide sufficient information to ensure conformity among different subunits. This is true whether the interactions are due to coupling or use of common resources (see page 22). If two subunits are closely coupled, their separate actions must be constrained to the extent necessary to ensure that their actions mesh with one another. The production rate of the manufacturing department must be consistent, for instance, with the marketing plan.

Similarly, the plans of subunits that draw from the same pool of a common resource must be constrained in a way that results in an efficient allocation of the resource. The more specific the resource, the more detailed the constraints. Long-range investment funds require less detailed higher-level allocation than, say, the scheduling of common manufacturing capacity among two product departments.

In some cases, a common resource is provided as a means of gaining the advantage of specialization. For example, an organization might establish a centralized information systems group that provides shared computer facilities and software systems. This may require that certain constraints be imposed on lower-level units if the organization as a whole is to reap the benefits of this specialization. For example, all units might be compelled to use common computer software.

Constraints imposed to resolve interactions lead to behavior that only approximates the global optimum. This is so because determining optimal constraints is, in general, equivalent to determining optimal actions throughout the organization.[11] If this information were available, the actions themselves, rather than constraints on lower-level planners, should probably be transmitted.

Therefore, a high-level planner normally cannot know the detailed ramifications of the constraints he imposes; at best he can consider the significant *aggregate* effects. The results of higher-level resolution of interactions are communicated as plans. A lower-level planner then tries to meet his assigned plan as best he can. If the plan is a good one, only insignificant penalties of suboptimization are introduced. This scheme thus provides a means of recognizing important interactions, while at the same time allowing each planner to formulate his plans without considering the detailed actions of others.

Even if it is infeasible to formulate higher-level plans that explicitly consider all important interactions simultaneously, lower-level planners should still have some information about the expected behavior of closely related units. For example, it may not be possible to determine an optimum plant-wide schedule, but a subassembly planner must know the assembly schedule before he can establish his own schedule. In other words, even if the magnitude of the task prevents a higher-level planner from treating lower-level actions as variables, a lower-level planner should at least for-

---

[11] However, an iterative process, in which goals of lower-level planners are adjusted sequentially in a way that the combined actions of the planners converge on a global optimum, may not require detailed knowledge of each subunit's activities (Arrow, 1959). Decomposition algorithms for solving large linear programming models formalize this process.

mulate his own plans with some knowledge about the value of the interface variables through which he interacts with other units.[12]

Figure 5-1 illustrates the way in which higher-level plans constrain lower-level planning. Suppose that a manufacturing company determines quarterly production schedules centrally as a means of coordinating production among interacting plants. The centralized scheduling might consider such things as the location and costs of various sources of raw material, the

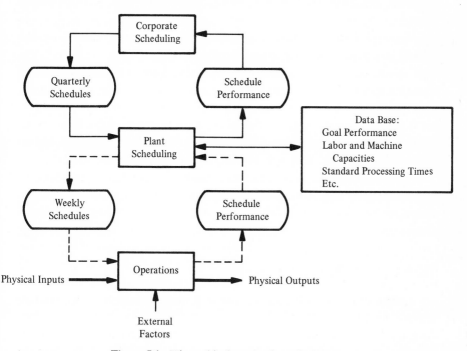

Figure 5-1. Hierarchical production scheduling

[12] In a purely competitive economy, interactions are resolved in the market place. Adam Smith's "invisible hand," acting through the price mechanism, provides the "higher-level" constraints within which each firm attempts to optimize. If significant interactions—or *externalities*—exist, then prices alone do not contain enough information to achieve an efficient allocation of resources (in the Pareto sense). Additional information might be provided, for example, by a central planning agency that assigns production quotas. But even if this "solution" were politically acceptable, the technical and computational problems involved make it infeasible under most circumstances.

The transfer prices associated with the movement of goods within a single firm serve an analogous role. They also suffer from the same shortcomings. Within the firm, however, interactions are likely to be relatively more significant, and higher-level planning as a means of coping with them becomes more feasible.

location of markets, production costs and capacities at each plant, and transportation costs. The resulting plant schedules presumably represent the firm's attempt to optimize overall production.

Within the constraints imposed by its quarterly schedule, each plant then determines weekly schedules over the course of the current quarter. Plant scheduling takes account of assigned goals (for example, achieve standard costs subject to quality and delivery standards), current machine and labor capacities, the estimated processing costs for each product, and so forth.

Finally, weekly schedules constrain actual operations. Guided by the weekly schedules, operating units transform physical inputs—material, energy, labor, and so on—into finished physical outputs. This may require the breaking down of weekly schedules into much more detailed plans. If, for example, the production process is controlled completely automatically by a "closed-loop" system, ultimately plans are expressed in the form of the required operating conditions (temperatures, flow rates, pressures, and so forth) to be maintained by a monitoring computer (Williams, 1968).

At each stage in the process performance information is fed back to higher-level planning agencies. If deviations become large enough, replanning may be required in order to alter planned activity in light of current conditions.

The Need for Higher-Level Constraints

The strong downward bias of planning in the presence of interactions suggests that the more critical issues are resolved at the higher-level planning stages and that the success of the organization depends less and less on plans generated at lower and lower levels. If this were not the case, the lowest levels could plan their own destiny unconstrained by higher-level considerations.

The behavior of an organization ultimately depends, of course, on the composite activity at its lowest levels. However, if the organization as a whole is to achieve purposeful behavior in the face of interactions, lower-level activity must be guided by a hierarchy of higher-level planning constraints. Otherwise, lower-level success tends to be local rather than global. For want of a nail a kingdom may be lost, but the best way to reduce this risk is to develop an improved inventory control system. Generals may organize logistic operations; they do not serve as blacksmiths.

To be sure, planning information has an upward as well as a downward flow. A higher-level plan may seemingly be generated merely as a composite of lower-level plans. Moreover, a higher-level planner is partially constrained by the information fed to him by the lower levels—like the "absolute" monarch effectively controlled by his ministers through their filtering of information made available to him. However, through a planner's control over aggregate resources and the specification of procedures used by the lower levels, he has considerable power over the plans and information reaching him. Furthermore, he retains the ultimate power of veto over proposed plans. This represents a potent instrument for guiding lower-level planning.[13]

Adaptation Through Hierarchical Planning

Conceptually, the hierarchy of planning can continue indefinitely. Every planning process is subject to constraints of one sort or another. These constraints are imposed by higher-level processes that are themselves subject to constraints. For example, the generation of an inventory plan is subject to constraints imposed by the particular computational algorithms used. The search for improved algorithms itself involves a form of planning. This planning is in turn subject to constraints. For instance, an operations research group developing inventory procedures is constrained by its organizational structure, goals, resource budget, information, policies, and procedures. We could develop in this manner still higher-level planning processes (procedures to change procedures to change procedures, say).

The organization can improve its behavior by making appropriate adjustments to constraints through a continual process of hierarchical adaptation. The adjustments should normally be small and evolutionary in order to increase the stability of planning. To the extent that the organization can discern the effects of changes, those adjustments that bring improvements can be continued and strengthened, and those that worsen behavior can be rescinded (hopefully with not too great a loss). Adaptation is thus essentially a search process (Morris, 1968, pp. 11–14).

[13] A planner with veto power acts, in effect, as a *trainer,* exercising his authority through selective *reinforcement* of lower-level behavior. He *rewards* a planning process by accepting its output, and *extinguishes* a process by rejecting its plans (Minsky, 1961, pp. 426–430). This mechanism offers the distinct advantage of not requiring the higher-level planner to have detailed knowledge of lower-level activities; he must only possess a means of distinguishing "acceptable" from "unacceptable" plans. Its great disadvantage is that it may be a much less efficient method of guiding lower-level behavior than more direct intervention. With only *go, no-go* information, lower-level units may move very slowly—if at all—towards improved planning. In practice, of course, additional information is provided in the form of specific requests for modifications to plans, veto messages, and so forth.

The frequency of adjustment varies with hierarchical level. A high-level constraint—such as organization structure and goals—requires infrequent changes, whereas low-level procedures may be revised relatively often (see page 32.) (Simon, 1962, p. 477; Mesarovic, 1962, p. 18). Each execution of a planning cycle provides little evidence for making changes in the process, especially in the presence of random variations. Since high-level planning ordinarily has a relatively long cycle time, changes in high-level planning constraints should be correspondingly infrequent. The stability thus provided contributes to the predictability of behavior and allows time for persons within the organization to learn their jobs and specialize their activities (Zannetos, 1965; Branch, 1966, p. 217).

The notion that adaptation comes through changes in the planning process has exceedingly important implications for management. If a manager hopes to exert a lasting and fundamental influence over the behavior of the organization, he must do it primarily through improvements in the planning process. He should not focus attention on *ad hoc* adjustments to plans, but rather on the process that generates the plans (and with the process that generated *that* process). In other words, he should concern himself with the cause of inadequate planning and not its symptoms.

5.4 *The Iterative Nature of Planning*

Consistency Among Hierarchical Plans

A higher-level plan affects actual behavior only indirectly through lower-level planning; it is only at the lowest level that plans directly guide actual operations. A higher-level plan therefore induces intended behavior only if lower-level plans are consistent with it. The organization must, therefore, rely on hierarchical consistency in order to achieve purposeful behavior directed toward the accomplishment of its global objectives.

Consistency must also be maintained across hierarchical lines. The interdependent nature of organizations makes it essential that significant conflicts should not arise between interacting plans. For example, the resource inputs and outputs incorporated in the plans of a manufacturing department should mesh in quantity and time phasing with the plans of the purchasing, personnel, and sales departments. The generation of a set of plans meeting all consistency requirements represents one of the major difficulties of planning.

Consistency among plans requires realistic planning and a control system that encourages compliance with plans. Without these, no logical assurance exists that consistency can or will be achieved. Conceivably, a higher-level plan may be completely infeasible, and therefore no feasible lower-level plan can be consistent with it.

Realism in planning can be achieved in two ways. The most common approach is to generate plans that differ only modestly from previous plans formulated under similar conditions. The continuity thus provided enormously simplifies high-level planning, since it permits the formulation of plans with a minimum amount of information—namely, information about past performance and the significant internal or external changes that have occurred subsequently (Cyert and March, 1963, pp. 111–112). (Determining the implications of such changes may be exceedingly difficult, however.)

Unfortunately, such conservatism bars the possibility of obtaining really fundamental improvements. To overcome this disadvantage, the planner must make a more far-reaching search for improved plans. To achieve realism with this more radical approach, the planner can no longer rely principally on information about past performance; he must have access to a much larger source of information in order to determine the probable consequences of untried plans.

In order to formulate a realistic plan, a high-level planner must be able to assess the detailed implications of different alternatives. Normally, the information-handling capacity available to him precludes such analysis, because otherwise it would be unnecessary to fragment the total planning task into lower-level components. He must therefore choose a plan without detailed consideration of the lower-level plans used to implement it. Thus, *strategists* can only assume "reasonable" performance on the part of *tacticians* in conformity with higher-level constraints (Starr, 1964, pp. 67–75).

The Need for Iterative Modification of Plans

Ignoring details can often lead to significant errors in high-level plans. Within the limits of his available information-handling capacity, a high-level planner must find a means of generating plans that consider detailed matters. This can be done most efficiently through an iterative dialogue with lower-level planners.

The iterative cycle starts with the formulation of a high-level preliminary plan. With this plan as a guide, lower-level planners can then propose plans that they consider realistic (perhaps as a result of proposals submitted to them by planners at still lower levels). The higher-level planner may modify such proposals, but hopefully in a way that does not do violence to their realism. The iterative process continues until "convergence" is achieved within required tolerances.

The great advantages of the iterative scheme is that it provides an efficient means of transferring planning information between hierarchical levels. On the one hand, a lower-level planner receives information by means of a provisional high-level plan. He can therefore confine his search for a detailed plan to those alternatives that appear consistent with higher-level goals. A high-level planner, on the other hand, receives information about detailed tradeoffs submerged from his view at the time he formulates his provisional plan. Upon closer lower-level scrutiny, a plan that appeared attractive in terms of the low-resolution, high-level planning model may be revealed to be unrealistic or undesirable in some respect.

Often the iterative nature of planning is not made explicit. In order to generate realistic plans through an explicit iterative process, lower-level planners have the responsibility to point out the tradeoffs implied by higher-level constraints. If the planning system is strongly biased against an upward flow of information, the organization will end up with plans that are either inconsistent or that ignore desirable tradeoffs. The lower levels may bury the inconsistencies by an elaborate shuffling of their resources, by bookkeeping sleight-of-hand, or by postponing as long as possible the inevitable day of reckoning. When the deviations finally do come to light, an inordinate amount of bureaucratic effort may go into a quest for excuses and alibis.[14]

Budgeting in the Defense Department illustrates the concept of iterative planning. The first step in the cycle involves the specification of preliminary budget "guidelines" for each of the military services. These guidelines are not intended to impose strict constraints on lower-level budgeting, but they do reflect national priorities established by basic military, political, and economic policy decisions made at the highest level in the government.

The military services budget their more detailed activities within the loose constraints imposed by the funding guidelines (as well as any other constraints on specific programs). The resulting proposed budgets may exceed the preliminary estimate, but presumably not by an unreasonable

---

[14] The issue, of course, is not as clear cut as might be implied. A lower-level planner obviously has his own biases, and probably they do not run in favor of a plan that presses him too energetically. A certain amount of gaming takes place when planners negotiate. Stedry (1962) discusses some of the issues involved.

amount. Any proposed increment to the budget provides tradeoff information based on the detailed knowledge available within a military service. Higher-level planners (for example, the Secretary of Defense, the President, or Congress) then must weigh the tradeoffs presented and choose a suitable balance among national goals. The final budget is ultimately reached through a complicated series of iterative negotiations (Burkhead, 1956, pp. 88–94).

Thus, despite the primacy of higher-level plans, it is nevertheless true that good planning cannot consist solely of either a downward or an upward flow of information and constraints. Both flows are necessary. It is primarily through an iterative exchange of information among levels that the organization can converge on a superior plan.[15]

5.5 *Geometric Interpretation of Planning*

It is perhaps useful to give a geometric interpretation to planning (Sisson, 1960, pp. 113–115; Manheim, 1964). In such terms, composite lowest-level plans constitute a point in an *n*-dimensional abstract space containing all alternative plans open to the organization.[16] Each detailed decision or outcome variable used to describe a plan (including those variables used to measure the uncertainty of the plan) represents a dimension of this space.

Every point has an associated utility value, a function of the variables that serve to define the point. Each point need not have a unique utility, and so two or more points may be indistinguishable from the standpoint of the goals of the planner.

A high-level plan defines a relatively large set of points that are consistent with its specified aggregate, low-resolution variables. In general, not all points included in such a set have the same utility. Therefore, a high-level plan typically does not have a single utility value, but rather a distribution of values (Manheim, 1964, p. 48).

The utility ultimately achieved depends on the way in which a high-level plan is elaborated into the lowest-level plans. Typically this information is not available to the high-level planner at the time he selects an alternative.

---

[15] Here, as in all matters concerned with the design of information systems, one must balance the value versus the cost of iterative revisions. Increased iterations add to cost as well as value. Furthermore, each iteration may take considerable time. Both costs and time thus limit the amount of revision that should take place.

[16] The plan space does not include all "real" alternatives, but only those that can be described in terms of the abstract variables used in formulating plans.

He must therefore make a choice (probably not consciously) on the basis of a subjective estimate of the probability distribution of utility values associated with each alternative high-level plan. The hierarchical planning process then successively narrows down the set of points remaining in the region constrained by higher-level plans. Ultimately, there remains only a single point having a single utility value (but which reflects, of course, the probabilistic nature of outcomes and the planner's attitude toward risk and uncertainty).

For a plan to be perfectly consistent with a higher-level plan, it must lie wholly within the region of the latter. Therefore, a set of consistent hierarchical plans is represented by a set of nested regions and a point in the innermost region associated with the most detailed plan. A higher-level region serves merely to confine the next lower-level region, which in turn confines the next region, and so on down to the most detailed plan. It is this detailed plan that guides behavior during the actual execution of a hierarchy of plans.

Because of the aggregate, low-resolution nature of high-level planning, a high-level planner does not know the precise set of points implied by a given plan. He may, in fact, select a high-level plan that is totally infeasible, or one that has unsuspected and undesirable consequences. In general, the high-level planner cannot include sufficient information within his planning model to guard against all possibility of overlooking important factors. He must rely, therefore, on iterative modifications of his plan to eliminate significant distortions caused by his gross model.

The total planning process involves a hierarchical search through the organization's *plan space*. A higher-level planning model deals in aggregates and gross approximations, and therefore the space of its perceived alternatives is much smaller than that of its composite lower-level models. (It is, however, still much too enormous to be explored exhaustively.) Within this space, the high-level planner employs a sequential search in order to locate a region having a high utility (at least in terms of the variables used in high-level planning). The success of the search process rests on the usefulness of information acquired through preceding probes of the space in directing the planner to regions with improved outcomes.

The hierarchical search process makes the total planning task both feasible and efficient by permitting each planner to concentrate on relatively small and independent aspects of the global problem. The use of a sequential search adds to the efficiency of the process, since each probe furnishes information useful for making further probes. The iterative nature of the process allows higher-level planning to deal with aggregate factors, on the assumption that any significant issues submerged from view of the high-level models will be revealed by the more detailed lower-level models.

5.6 *The Planning Process at a Given Level*

Conceptually, the steps involved in generating a plan are largely independent of the level in the planning hierarchy at which it takes place. To be sure, the scope and degree of aggregation vary greatly among levels. Furthermore, high-level planning is typically much less clearly defined and structured than low-level planning. Nevertheless, in order to provide an overall view of the process, it seems useful to stress similarities rather than differences among levels (although one must not ignore the rather important differences that exist, as Anthony [1965, p. 116] points out).

Planning that takes place at any level in the hierarchy is triggered in different ways. It may be performed at fixed intervals, as in the case of preparing annual budgets or weekly production schedules. In this case, the planning is triggered in sufficient time to meet plan deadlines. Alternatively, planning may be initiated as a result of some event, such as the arrival of a sales order, the breakdown of a machine, the reporting of a significant deviation from an existing plan, a change in sales strategy on the part of a competitor, or the revision of a higher-level plan. Finally, planning may take place not in response to a particular event, but rather as a means of improving present performance or capabilities. Such planning may arise from a change in underlying economic conditions or technology, or simply through the recognition of a long-existing opportunity.

The triggering of planning sets off an enormously complex process. No mere description can do full justice to its complexity. However, the following sequence of steps, though admittedly somewhat arbitrary and simplified, hopefully captures the essential character of the process.

Determine Primitive Planning Data

The first step in planning is to determine the values of the primitive or basic data to be used. These planning data (or planning *factors* in military terminology) constitute the building blocks from which plans are generated (Goetz, 1949, pp. 92–115).

The nature of the "primitive" data depends on the level of the planning hierarchy. Primitive data for a low-level process are typically much more detailed than those used in high-level planning. For example, a planner in a maintenance department might formulate his budget using such data as the costs of various types of supplies and the wage rate of different grades of labor, while a manufacturing division might budget maintenance costs on the basis of the ratio of past costs to total dollar production.

Often primitive planning data at one level are derived as a result of more detailed planning at lower levels. For instance, a figure for the average wage rate used in corporate planning may be derived from a detailed lower-level analysis. Higher-level plans also constitute primitive data for lower-level processes. For example, a quarterly production schedule, existing capacity constraints, and an allowed scrap rate all represent primitive data for generating weekly production schedules.

Primitive planning data are not mere "facts" retrieved from the organization's data base. Facts are always historical, and planning involves the future. Obviously, the future can be predicted only on the basis of information about the past, but the transformation of historical data into predicted values of planning data may involve a complex series of operations. An elaborate regression analysis might be used in sales forecasting, for example. Sometimes past data also call for "normalization" in order to wash out the effects of nonstandard conditions prevailing in the past.

Any prediction is, of course, subject to error. When outcomes are insensitive to random variability of primitive data, the information system need only provide point predictions. This greatly reduces the amount of data storage and computation required for prediction and vastly simplifies the subsequent use of the predictions in planning. If point estimates are not sufficient, the information system must provide additional data about variability in the form of interval estimates, estimates of variance or other parameters of probability distributions, or conceivably even a complete history of individual events (see pages 43–44).

A given planning process has an associated *planning horizon* over which predictions are made. The length of this time period depends very much on the nature of the planning process.

Consider sales forecasts, for example. A grocery store receiving daily off-the-truck delivery of bakery goods need forecast individual product demand only over a one-day horizon. The bakery, on the other hand, might forecast product demand over a three-day period in order to allow for scheduling and manufacturing lead times. In scheduling labor-force requirements it may have to forecast over a two-week horizon for products aggregated by their labor content. (For example, white and whole wheat bread may be lumped together, since they have virtually the same labor content, while a distinction must be made between bread and cakes.) The horizon for ordering flour may extend over a month, and decisions regarding additions to oven capacity may call for a horizon of several years.

The appropriate planning horizon is governed to a considerable extent by the design of the planning process. The more frequent the replanning, the shorter the horizon. Short-interval periodic planning, or planning with tight control limits, thus offer the great advantage of shortening the prediction span as a means of improving the accuracy of predictions over the horizon. Each replanning cycle provides an opportunity at least partially to correct for earlier errors. Even in cases where a cycle is not independent because of the residual effects of decisions made during earlier cycles, the weight given to future periods tends to drop off sharply past a few periods. This is true, for instance, of work-force planning, in which a cost is incurred when changes are made to the employment level (Holt *et al.*, 1960, p. 118).

Once planning data have been determined, their predicted values should remain in effect over the prediction span or until feedback data from the control system provide clear evidence that the predictions are in significant error. Thus, feedback data are not used directly in planning, but only indirectly through the prediction process. The prediction process, in turn, filters out much of the noise contained in the feedback data, and thereby stabilizes plans.

Propose Alternative Plans and Generate Their Predicted Outcomes

The second step in planning is the manipulation of the primitive planning data in order to determine the consequences of alternative plans. Each plan considered is described by means of its decision variables, and the consequences stemming from these decisions are described in terms of outcome variables.

A planner is normally responsible for generating alternatives. This is especially true of high-level planning, in which the variety of alternatives is typically so vast and so little understood that the generation process cannot be formalized to the extent that human participation is not required. If, however, a planning process can be highly formalized, alternatives may be generated automatically. In the simplex algorithm for solving linear programming problems, for instance, alternatives are generated in a way that guarantees that the latest one is at least as good (in terms of a linear payoff function) as the alternatives generated earlier. Even when a feasible optimizing algorithm is not available, a formalized search strategy can sometimes be used to probe for "near optimal" plans if there exist an objective function and a model for determining the outcome variables associated with a given alternative (Wilde, 1964; Taubert, 1968).

Only recognized alternatives can eventually be selected for execution, and only a minute fraction of possible alternatives can typically be considered explicitly. Therefore, a planner's effectiveness depends heavily on his ability to apply subtle heuristics in limiting detailed examination to a small number of good alternatives. The problem of overlooking outstanding alternatives is by no means absent even when an "optimizing" algorithm is employed, because the algorithm can only find the best alternative out of the set permitted by the formal model.

The transformation of decision variables into outcome variables always requires some sort of model. This is true whether the planner uses a formalized model—expressed perhaps in the form of mathematical equations or a computer simulation program—or informal, "back of the envelope" methods. In every case he must rely on an abstract representation of reality (Craik, 1943, p. 61; Boulding, 1956, p. 14). Planning models of course vary greatly in their degree of accuracy in predicting outcomes, in their complexity and completeness, and in their formality. High-level models are typically informal and ill structured, whereas low-level models often permit considerable formalization.

Select the "Best" Alternative

From the list of alternatives generated and analyzed in the previous step, the plan that appears most suitable should be selected. This choice is governed by the goals that have been assigned by a higher-level planning process. If there exists a single measurable goal, one can simply choose the plan that leads to the best performance in terms of the goal. This, of course, will not represent the "optimum" plan unless *all* alternatives either have been considered explicitly or have been rejected by some logical means as being inferior to the set considered. The true—but unknown—optimum recognizes the cost of searching for improved alternatives, and therefore rejects a stubborn hunt for the "perfect" plan.

For the reasons discussed earlier (see page 115) a single goal rarely exists. Rather, a planner normally faces multiple goals and uncertain consequences of his actions. Under these circumstances, the decision process becomes very much more complex than merely choosing the alternative having the highest utility in terms of a single goal.

When facing uncertainty[17] and multiple goals, one cannot, in general, find a dominant alternative that is best along all goal dimensions. If such a situation existed, it would generally be advantageous to explore more alternatives (perhaps in the "region" of the dominant alternative) in order to probe for the *efficiency frontier,* along which the improvement in one goal dimension implies a worsening in one or more other dimensions (Hitch and McKean, 1960, pp. 109–114).

Figure 5-2 illustrates this concept. Suppose an inventory planner has two goals: reduce the aggregate inventory investment and reduce the stock-out rate. Suppose further that he has generated alternatives *A, B,* and *C.* In this case he would clearly choose alternative *A,* since it dominates the other two. However, further exploration might reveal alternatives *D* and *E,* which are not dominated by *A* and therefore call for a hard choice in trading off improvement in one dimension at the sacrifice of poorer performance in the other.

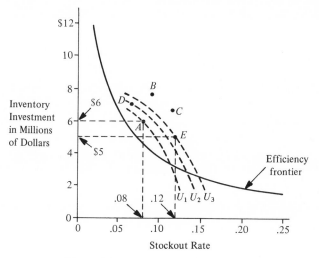

Figure 5-2. Choice of alternative plans

The efficiency frontier, by definition, defines the set of feasible alternatives consistent with current technology and physical constraints. In Figure 5-2, all feasible points lie to the right of the curve. The frontier is generally

[17] Decision making under uncertainty can be viewed as a special case of decision making with multiple goals. The measures of uncertainty—probability or variance estimates, for example—constitute an additional dimension by which a plan is described.

not known, and available alternatives do not exhaust all possibilities for improvement. However, the cost of probing for improved plans may exceed the expected gain (at least in the opinion of the planner), and therefore the planner might settle for a choice among alternatives *A, D,* and *E* (alternatives *B* and *C* being dismissed because of their dominance by *A*).

In resolving a choice that involves a tradeoff among multiple goals, the planner might specify an explicit utility function that transforms all goals into a single compound goal (Klahr, 1958; Ackoff, 1962, pp. 42–44). Once this has been done, the choice becomes a trivial one: select the alternative with the highest utility in terms of the compound goal. In Figure 5-2, a utility function is plotted in the form of three contour lines, U_1, U_2, and U_3, that pass through the alternatives *A, D,* and *E*. All points lying on a given contour have the same utility. (These contours are, of course, the well-known *indifference curves* of the economist.) The contour line closest to the origin clearly has the highest utility, and so alternative *A* is the one selected out of the known alternatives available.

The specification of the explicit utility function obviously represents the critical step in the selection analysis. The function must embody the planner's "true" goals (and those of higher-level planners). In most cases these goals are extremely difficult to describe in analytical form.[18] A formal description would have to recognize the complex and subtle interactions that may occur among goals. For example, if the survival of the organization is not threatened, the organization can indulge in research and development projects, improvements in the corporate image, added security and benefits for its employees, and other such future-directed goals of the affluent organization. If, however, the life of the organization (or the planner's existence within the organization) is at stake, then all other goals tend to be forgotten in a single-minded preoccupation with survival.

An attempt to develop a comprehensive explicit utility function may prove fruitful in guiding decisions and providing insights. However, it is unlikely to do more than that, at least in the case of higher-level planning. The planner typically does not know enough about his utility function to formalize it completely (see page 115), and he obviously cannot defer decisions until he does. Different goals are often hopelessly incommensurable (in the sense that no generally agreed tradeoff exists among them); in this case, a spurious tradeoff function suppresses information about alternative

---

[18] The difficulty in specifying a planner's utility function should not be too surprising. If the function could be captured once and for all in analytical form, one of the primary responsibilities of the manager would be eliminated: any clerk or computer can rank a series of single-dimensional numbers.

plans instead of simplifying the selection process (Hitch and McKean, 1960, p. 185). Moreover, goals tend to change frequently enough that an explicit utility function would often be obsolete by the time it had been developed.

Nevertheless, some formalization is extremely useful, and indeed necessary. Even if all goals cannot be collapsed into a single compound utility function, their number can be reduced through the use of a tradeoff function among subsets of the goals. Without this compression, the planner would be swamped with an unmanageable abundance of competing goals.[19] For example, in evaluating alternative aircraft designs, it may be possible to achieve a fairly general consensus about the tradeoffs between various performance variables such as speed, range, altitude, rate of climb, and payload. By use of the tradeoff transformation, each alternative design can be assigned a single index of performance. Similar indices might be developed for "cost" and "logistic support," say. The final choice of design is thus reduced to the comparison of alternatives described in terms of three incommensurable composite dimensions rather than a whole host of detailed dimensions.

Hierarchical aggregation of management information also illustrates the concept of goal compression. A particularly simple tradeoff function is typically used: all variables within an aggregation are considered equivalent, or at most a weighting factor (dollar value, say) is applied to each of the different variables. Sales performance, for instance, may be reported at the lowest level by salesman and individual item. These detailed data may then be combined into state, regional, and national totals in increasingly large aggregations. The subtotals available at each level presumably correspond to the goals appropriate to that level.

Simple aggregation as a means of compressing goals may hide significant information about the variables aggregated. An aggregate inventory goal, for example, may wash out the fact that some items have a large surplus in inventory, while others are critically short. Similarly, setting a delivery-performance goal merely in terms of the number of overdue customer orders does not differentiate between orders that are one day late and those that are, say, five weeks late. These problems can be eliminated by a change in the tradeoff function used. Inventory items can, for example, be classified as "surplus," "short," or "within control," and inventory goals can then be

---

[19] Haberstroh (1958, 68–69) concludes that any stable organization can deal with only a relatively small number of mutually independent goals. Schleh (1961, pp. 22–23) suggests no more than five separate goals should be assigned. These conclusions are consistent with Miller's result (1956).

expressed in terms of the aggregate inventory within each of these classifications. Delivery performance can be measured by weighting each overdue order according to the amount of time it is late.

In order to guard against washing out relevant information during goal compression, a planner should be permitted to examine the separate components of a composite goal. Thus, the decision maker selecting an aircraft design might want to look at separate performance characteristics, and a national sales manager might want to examine the detailed sales within any region that is not meeting its sales goal. The ability to trace the cause of major deviations through a hierarchical search of the details should be incorporated within any information system.

Compression of goals can be achieved by reducing the resolution used in measuring goal variables. For example, inventory investment could be rounded to the nearest million dollars. Two plans might therefore differ in inventory by almost a million dollars and still be indistinguishable in terms of the inventory goal.

A constraint can be viewed as a special type of low-resolution utility function that distinguishes between only two values for a given goal, "acceptable" or "not acceptable." Thus, a planner might establish a constraint of $5 million on inventory; plans involving a projected inventory investment exceeding this figure would therefore be rejected. If all goal dimensions except one are constrained in this manner, the selection of a plan is reduced to choosing the acceptable alternative having the highest rating in terms of the remaining goal. If constraints are attached to *all* dimensions, the planner follows a *satisficing* strategy and chooses the first alternative found that meets all constraints (March and Simon 1958, pp. 48–50 and 140–141).

The specification of constraints greatly simplifies the selection process by effectively eliminating the constrained dimensions from the evaluation of the alternatives that survive the constraints. However, the low resolution of constraints carries the risk of failing to distinguish between alternatives that differ significantly. Because of this, a plan that is distinctly superior to other alternatives except in a constrained dimension might be overlooked because it fails to meet the constraint. If the planner were confronted with an explicit tradeoff between the constrained dimension and the other dimensions, he might vastly prefer the rejected plan to all others (Hitch and McKean, 1960, p. 186). In Figure 5–2, for example, a $5 million constraint on the inventory investment causes the rejection of alternative *A* and the acceptance of *E*. However, if presented with the option of a decrease in the stockout rate from .12 to .08 at the penalty of an additional $1 million in inventory, the planner might well accept the tradeoff and choose plan *A*.

Even if a planner cannot specify an *explicit* utility function, he must still make a choice among alternatives on the basis of his assignment of *subjective* utility values. By so doing, he implicitly establishes bounds on the tradeoffs between goals. In the previous example, if the planner selects plan *A* in preference to plan *E*, he is implying that he is willing to increase inventory by *at least* $1 million in order to reduce the stockout rate from .12 to .08.[20] A tradeoff decision conveys less information than does the specification of an explicit utility function, and for this reason it is much easier to make. Whenever a planner selects a given plan, he should, of course, be made aware of the tradeoffs implied by his choice so that he can assess whether, in fact, the choice is consistent with his subjective utility function.

A subjective utility function, by its very nature, is ill defined. It is apt to change over time in response to changes in the planner's perceptions, insights, aspiration level, and "judgment." Furthermore, there is no reason to suppose that the planner always assigns consistent utilities (in the sense that they exhibit transitivity).[21]

Regardless of how the planner assigns utilities, he may decide that none of the alternatives currently available to him is acceptable. He may therefore generate and analyze additional alternatives. He will continue to do so until he feels that the cost of further search exceeds the expected improvement in utility that it will bring (Goetz, 1949, pp. 173–175).

Translate the Selected Plan into a Form for Lower-Level Planning

The variables used in planning need not be the same ones employed to communicate with other parts of the organization. For example, a planner might choose to aggregate variables before passing them down to lower-level planners. He might do this in the spirit of decentralization, relying on the lower-level planners to develop their own detailed plans constrained

---

[20] According to the explicit utility function shown in Figure 5-2, the planner would actually be willing to increase inventory by over $2 million in order to achieve the specified reduction in the stockout rate.

[21] Some "inconsistencies" may be more apparent than real. If the formal outcome variables do not include important but unquantified characteristics of a plan (pertaining to risk, say), then what appears to be formally "irrational" may merely reflect differences in the submerged variables (Bowman, 1963).

by aggregate variables that have been found feasible through a detailed analysis. On the other hand, it is difficult to see how a planner could reasonably assign more detailed constraints to lower-level planners than he himself used at his own planning level. Regardless of how the translation is performed, however, the end result should be a clear-cut assignment of responsibility for carrying out every portion of the total plan.

Control of the Plan

The final step in the planning process is the control of the approved plan. The control system compares actual performance against the plan. To the extent possible, the system should filter out the insignificant deviations and report only the significant ones requiring management attention. This can be done by establishing control tolerances for each relevant variable. Exception reports then identify deviations that exceed their limits.

The feedback information provided by the control system serves three important functions. For one thing, it encourages more realistic initial planning and closer adherence to approved plans. There is ample evidence to suggest that without adequate control, planning tends to become a superficial exercise.[22] Of course, encouragement to meet plans should not be so great as to motivate the lower levels to plan too conservatively or to persevere doggedly with an outmoded plan. The system should be such that it greatly discourages failure to acknowledge highly probable future deviations.

Secondly, the control system guards against excessive deviations from current plans that cause a partial breakdown in coordination. As deviations grow larger, the myriad interrelated activities throughout the organization soon get out of mesh. Furthermore, the cost of getting a plan back into control (for example, by the use of overtime to recover schedule slippage) may become large as deviations accumulate. The tighter the control limits, the sooner deviations are detected.

The control system should provide a hierarchy of responses to reported deviations. The lowest-level response is simply to ignore the deviation. Owing to the relatively unsophisticated nature of most control limits, a

---

[22] One need not search very far back within the archives of the Defense Department, for example, to discover past instances where original plans proved to be wildly unrealistic. Part of this is due to the advanced technology involved in modern weapons; but at least part of the blame rests with a system that positively encouraged overoptimistic initial plans and insufficiently discouraged cost escalations and schedule slippages. These problems have been widely recognized, of course, and many of them are currently being corrected.

deviation might be tagged as an exception when in fact the current plan should be retained (because the penalty of keeping it is less than the cost of any revision).

Alternatively, the current plan might be modified "locally" to the extent necessary to bring it back within control limits. The cost of such local replanning tends to be small. The disadvantage, however, is that once a deviation has occurred the current plan ceases, in general, to be the optimal one.

The highest-level form of response is a complete replanning that involves the same sequence of steps used in the creation of the existing plan. Such planning examines the current situation anew, constrained only by higher-level plans and the consequences stemming from past actions. Close scrutiny may, of course, reveal that the existing plan is still the best one currently available (even if, on hindsight, the existing plan should not have been adopted in the first place). If replanning indicates that the current plan should be revised, and if this then causes a deviation at the next higher level in the planning hierarchy, appropriate error signals should be sent to higher-level planners. Such exception reporting should continue on up the planning hierarchy to the point where deviations can be contained within existing control limits.

The level of response to an error signal depends on the seriousness of the deviation. The planner is clearly faced with a tradeoff decision aimed at balancing the cost of ignoring the deviation against the cost of revising the plan. The more serious the deviation, the more resources one should devote to replanning. The decision in most cases must be based on a subjective evaluation of the tradeoffs, because, paradoxically, the penalty of not revising the plan can only be established once the revised plan has been determined.

An example may be in order here. Suppose that a monthly production schedule has been determined for the next six months. Such a schedule is based on (among other things) predicted sales over the planning horizon. If, at the end of the first month, sales turn out to be 1,000 units less than predicted, the planner is faced with the following alternatives: (1) stick with the existing production schedule over the remaining five months; (2) cut back the second month's schedule by 1,000 units in order to bring inventories to their planned level at the end of the month; or (3) completely replan (including, perhaps, revision of the sales predictions) in order to determine the best schedule in light of current information. The proper response depends, of course, on the planner's estimates of the tradeoffs involved.

The final important function of the control system is to provide feedback information for adaptation. The control system should, when feasible, identify sources of (and responsibility for) deviations from plans in such a way that continual improvement can be made in the planning process. For example, the system might distinguish between deviations caused by errors in predicting basic planning data and those caused by errors in the planning model (Emery and Ness, 1968, Sect. 2.5). The identification and correction of deficiencies in the planning process provides the primary means by which the organization can achieve fundamental improvements through adaptation.[23]

5.7 *Economics of Planning*

Virtually every organization of any size engages in some formal planning, and no organization plans everything in the most minute detail. The issue is one of degree: what is the proper level of resources to devote to planning? The resolution of this question represents one of the more fundamental issues facing the organization.

Planning represents a "dry run" of organizational activities prior to their actual execution, and can thus be viewed as a form of simulation. From this simulation process emerges a network of plans that describes desired behavior on the part of all units within the organization. With the plans as a guide, then, the organization carries on activities that (hopefully) are directed toward the accomplishment of its global goals.

The value of a plan stems from the improvement it brings in the behavior of the persons whose actions it guides or constrains. This, in turn, depends on how closely the actions motivated by a plan correspond to optimal actions. Any plan suffers in some degree from the following imperfections: (1) the actions it describes are not the optimal ones; (2) the actions are not feasible, on account of overlooked physical constraints; and (3) the actions are described in sufficiently ambiguous terms to permit (that is, not be inconsistent with) nonoptimal behavior.

Tradeoffs exist among these three types of error. For example, as actions are described in greater detail, the probability increases that they will

[23] Adaptation can be viewed as a continuation of hierarchical control. Thus, if a serious deviation is signaled by the control system, replanning may call for the revision of not only the plan having the immediate deviation but also the model from which this plan was derived (representing a higher-level plan). The model may be revised through such means as changes in its parameters or, more fundamentally, in its basic structure. See page 156.

be neither optimal nor feasible. Conversely, as the constraints imposed by a plan are relaxed to permit greater lower-level flexibility, the likelihood increases that the optimal plan is included within the constraints.

Similar tradeoffs are effected by changing the hierarchical level at which planning takes place. It is easier to find feasible and detailed plans when they encompass a narrow scope. Such plans, however, are much less likely to approximate the global optimal plan for the organization (although they may achieve an optimum with respect to assigned subgoals). Higher-level planning can more closely approximate the global optimum, but with a loss of detail and a greater risk of infeasibility.

Additional resources devoted to planning serve to reduce planning errors. The resources include those associated with the processing of planning data, as well as personnel who design and implement the system. These resources can be employed in several different ways.

One way is to increase the scope of planning as a means of reducing interactions among subunits. Increased detail and complexity can also be employed to add realism to planning models. For example, one can substitute nonlinear relationships for linear ones, or treat variables as probabilistic rather than deterministic. Planning frequency can be increased by reducing the time interval between periodic replanning or by imposing tighter control limits. Finally, more alternatives can be generated and evaluated during each planning cycle in order to increase the expected quality of plans.

Factors Encouraging Planning

If a plan describes actions that are both detailed and feasible, lower-level planners may be motivated to abide by the plan whether or not they perceive it to be the best one possible. Under these circumstancs, any improvement that reduces the degree to which the plan deviates from the optimum has a value equal to the resulting increase in payoff. Conceptually, the problem facing the planner is simply to balance this value against the cost of any incremental resources devoted to planning.

The problem is conceptually more difficult if a plan is ambiguous, infeasible, or ignored in part by those responsible for executing it because they feel alternative actions are superior to the planned ones. Here the value of reducing planning errors depends on the quality of unplanned actions. If they approximate optimal behavior, then greater planning can contribute little value. If, on the other hand, actions taken without prior formal planning tend to be clearly inferior to planned actions, then additional planning may improve behavior substantially. This issue hinges on whether decisions formulated in a simulated planning world are superior to decisions made informally as actual events take place. The simulated world has at least three distinct advantages. Let us examine them.

Access to Increased Information-Handling Capacity. The ability of a person to choose an action in the absence of a formal plan is severely restricted by his limited information-handling capability. The relatively low capacity of his human sensory channels limits his ability to perceive the current state of the environment. His information storage is slow and unreliable. His modest computing power permits him to deal with only simple mental images of the real world.

A formal planner has available much greater information-handling capacity. He is not limited to his own human facilities, but can draw upon the aid of other persons. He can also use information-handling equipment and libraries of previously prepared computer programs. As a result, the planner can develop and manipulate formal models that take into account a great number of interacting variables. His behavior can therefore be based on a much more comprehensive picture of the world than the myopic view of the nonplanner.

A nonplanner is closely tied to real events, and his limited computing rate imposes a constraint on his ability to analyze a current situation. Time moves inexorably forward; it cannot be stopped to allow for additional gathering and processing of information before he must make an urgent decision.

Because the planner lives in a simulated world, he has much greater control over time than does his nonplanning counterpart. Simulated time moves as the planner directs. The time required to make a decision about a simulated event bears no relation to the time required to execute it. Therefore, a planner is constrained, not by his instantaneous information-processing rate, but rather by the total available processing capacity over the required planning response time.

The modest information-handling capacity available to the nonplanner limits his ability to make predictions about the future. The formal planner suffers from no such limitations, because in his simulated world the timing of an event can be specified. (The degree of correspondence between these *simulated* events and later *real* events is, of course, another matter, and represents the real test of the usefulness of planning.) By looking into the future, a planner can incorporate in a plan the current actions required to bring about desired future outcomes. In the absence of planning, allowance cannot be made for the lead times required to accomplish all of the antecedent steps.[24]

Evaluation of Alternatives.   The second advantage of planning is that simulated history is not irrevocable: The moving finger writes; and, having writ, may be cancelled. A planner can simply discard an alternative that fails to satisfy his goals, and can continue to generate plans until he finds it advantageous to stop.

The final plan that emerges from this process must, of course, be chosen from the set of alternatives considered. Therefore, for a given planning process, the larger the number of alternatives evaluated, the greater the expected payoff (Carroll, 1966, p. 48).

Simulation in an Abstract Space.   The third advantage of planning is that it deals with an explicit abstraction that greatly facilitates the process of searching for desirable outcomes. The variables used in planning furnish only the barest outline of the real world. The vast bulk of variables are omitted altogether or aggregated with other variables, most interactions are ignored, and functional relationships are greatly simplified. The resulting abstract model of the real world may be embodied in a formal mathematical or computer language, or in such forms as the conventional budgeting model.

The usefulness of these abstractions depends on the fulfillment of two requirements: (1) the planner must find the abstract world somehow more congenial to formulating satisfactory plans than he does the real world, and (2) a satisfactory plan in the abstract world must translate into satisfactory actions in the real world.

The first requirement offers no great problem. The real world is, by design, abstracted in a way and to a degree that allows the planner to manipulate the resulting model with relative ease. Within the abstract world, then, the planner searches for a satisfactory plan by whatever means seem appropriate. In particular, he might compute an optimum plan if his abstract model permits the application of available optimization techniques (and if it is optimal to compute the "optimum").

The second requirement presents more serious difficulties. The success of a plan hinges on whether it leads to satisfactory performance judged in "real" terms. The planner, in developing his abstraction of the real world,

---

[24] Experimental results in physical control systems demonstrate dramatically the importance of anticipating future actions (Sheridan *et al.,* 1964).

attempts to achieve a close correspondence between performance predicted by a plan and the resulting behavior in the real world. Only if his model passes this test will a "good" plan necessarily lead to good behavior. This is by no means a simple requirement.

The correspondence between a plan and the ultimate outcome achieved depends on three factors: (1) the realism of the model used to generate the plan, (2) the accuracy with which basic planning data are predicted, and (3) the fidelity with which the plan is carried out.

A planning model is realistic to the extent that the transformation of decisions into outcomes is the same in both the model and the real world. The relation between a planning model and the real world is diagrammed in Figure 5-3. Ideally, the model should represent a *homomorphism* of the real world. If it does, any set of actions consistent with a plan will result in the predicted outcomes as measured by the abstract outcome variables.

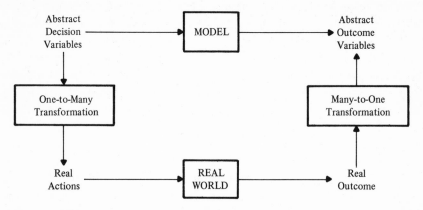

Figure 5-3. Correspondence between model and real world

The second factor affecting the correspondence between a plan and the eventual real outcome is the accuracy achieved in predicting values of the primitive planning data used in the planning model. Because of prediction errors, a model may provide a perfect structural homomorphism of the real world and yet fail to predict outcomes. This problem can be mitigated (if warranted by the economics of the situation) by increasing the accuracy of prediction through the use of more elaborate computation or by having more detailed and timely information; by maintaining a control system that quickly detects significant deviations from the most recent predictions; or, if the other approaches prove infeasible, by making structural changes in the real world (see page 97).

The outcome achieved ultimately rests on the persons responsible for executing a plan. Although good plans are often not followed with precision, the failure often lies in the plan's imperfections and not in human perversity. A plan obviously cannot be adhered to if it is infeasible. But a feasible plan is only a necessary condition, and not a sufficient one. An excellent plan can fail if it is not adhered to because of faulty communications, poor motivation, or other management shortcomings.

Job-shop scheduling illustrates these concepts. As a means of economizing on planning, an organization might use an overly simplified planning model—for example, the standard backdating scheme that implicitly assumes infinite capacity at each work center. Under these circumstances, the plan provides only a loose guide to action. It is therefore difficult to predict its precise effects. It will obviously have some influence on detailed dispatching decisions, but the process by which ambiguities are resolved often depends on a number of subtle factors.

Suppose, for example, that the schedule assigns to a machine more work than it can perform during a given time period. In this case, the original schedule cannot be executed as planned, and the dispatcher responsible for executing it must make some adjustments. He bases such decisions on his limited "local" perception of shop conditions and on the measures by which his performance is judged. His decision process might call for running the jobs in the *order* scheduled (but not at their scheduled *times*), or it may involve more complex considerations.

Given the unpredicted circumstances, it might very well be better if the dispatcher deviates from the job order originally scheduled. A critical job, for example, might be unduly delayed by a slavish adherence to the sequence specified in an obsolete schedule. The dispatcher's willingness to deviate from the scheduled sequence depends in part on the motivation exerted by the control system to conform to schedules even though they become clearly unrealistic. If strong motivation exists, plans can have the effect of decreasing flexibility (Hall, 1962, pp. 79–80).

Use of a more realistic planning model reduces problems of this sort. For example, a job-shop schedule might be generated through a detailed simulation of the shop (Emery, 1961; Carroll, 1965). However, even though the model itself may be an accurate abstraction, the predicted values of capacities and processing times may be—and, in general, will be—somewhat in error. As a result, the shop may not be able to follow the schedule precisely. Hopefully, however, the predictions will be good enough that the schedule serves as an operationally feasible guide between planning intervals. The extent to which the schedule "decays" (that is, becomes unrealistic) toward the end of an interval depends on the length of the interval and the predictability of planning data. A highly uncertain environment may call for an on-line, real-time scheduling system that is capable of rescheduling any time a significant, unanticipated event occurs (for example, a machine breakdown) (Carroll, 1967a).

Factors Limiting Planning

It is, of course, exceedingly difficult to assess the marginal value and cost of additional planning in arriving at an optimum planning system (see Section 4.3). Nevertheless, the planner cannot avoid making at least a subjective assessment. In doing this, it is well for him to keep in mind the limitations of planning.

The basic limitation is the uncertainty associated with the predicted values of planning data. Uncertainty exists about such matters as competitors' strategies, future technological developments, and the value of variables subject to random fluctuations (Hitch and McKean, 1960, p. 188–192).

The organization has several ways of dealing with uncertainty. It can, for example, make structural changes in the environment that reduce uncertainty or render payoff less sensitive to uncertainty. This can be done through various decoupling devices, general-purpose resources, and certain institutional arrangements that create a "negotiated environment" (such as a long-term contract that fixes the price for a basic raw material) (Cyert and March, 1963, p. 120). The organization can also devote more effort to collecting and processing information in order to improve predictions. It can use sequential decision making, short planning cycles, and a control system that provides rapid feedback as a means of reducing the planning horizon over which predictions must be made.

Planning models can be used to provide information about the sensitivity of outcomes to uncertainty. Instead of using single estimates for planning data, a range of estimates might be employed. The planner can then assess the outcomes of alternative plans under varying degrees of pessimism or optimism.

Reduction of uncertainty is not achieved without a cost. Risks transferred in an effort to achieve a negotiated environment must be assumed by someone else, and this person must be compensated for his risk-taking. Flexibility in resources adds to their cost. Increased sophistication in predicting planning data increases data-processing costs. And explicit consideration of multiple values of planning data increases factorially the number of alternatives that must be evaluated (Hitch and McKean, 1960, p. 193).

Response-time requirements can also impose severe limitations on the amount of planning that can be performed. Under some circumstances it is better to take quick action rather than take the time to do a more thorough job of planning. This problem can be reduced by preparing several alternative contingency plans that deal with the various situations that may arise. This adds considerably to the cost of planning, however, and requires that there exist only a relatively few different situations that must be anticipated.

The ultimate limitation on planning is, of course, its cost. Diminishing returns eventually set in as additional resources are spent on planning. Furthermore, costs tend to increase more than proportionally as additional variables, relationships, and complexities are introduced. There soon comes the point at which it is cheaper to muddle through with a somewhat ambiguous and unrealistic plan than it is to reduce its imperfections.

5.8 *Man–Machine Planning*

The planning process discussed up to this point represents a conceptual viewpoint largely independent of the methods used to implement it. The final topic to be considered is the role that computers might play in this process, particularly at the higher levels within the organization. The discussion is necessarily somewhat speculative, and is therefore no doubt subject to the usual hazards of speculation: wild, unsupported fancies and pious hopes on the one hand, and unimaginative commonplaces on the other. I shall try my best to avoid these risks.

There seems to be a general consensus that computers will contribute increasingly to planning at all levels. Nevertheless, skeptics certainly have no difficulty in marshalling ample empirical evidence to support a less sanguine view. The results achieved to date in using computers in higher-level planning processes have been relatively drab and meager compared with their widespread use for low-level operational planning (Deardon, 1964).

None of this experience supports a view that inherent limitations preclude the use of computers in higher-level planning. Developing formal computer models to aid the planner obviously presents a task of great difficulty—but not a unique one. A planner cannot avoid the use of a model, whether he relies on a formalized model or his own intuition. There is every reason to suppose that formalized computer models can improve the planning process. Without such aid, the planner is easily flooded by the immense quantities of data involved in planning and by the complexity stemming from interacting variables.

Capabilities of Man and the Machine

The use of computers in planning certainly does not imply that the planner must abdicate his responsibilities to the machine. In order to make a major improvement in the planning process, we will have to draw upon the best features of both man and machine.

Listing the relative advantages of man versus the machine has become a popular sport.[25] Such a comparison depends greatly upon the current state of technology: the supposed advantages of man tend to diminish as technology advances. Nevertheless, man as an information processor does currently enjoy a number of advantages over the computer, and will doubtlessly hold this edge for some time to come.

Man's superiority lies primarily in his ability to recognize subtle patterns, to recall relevant information through association, to learn, and to exercise intelligence and originality. Even in cases in which the computer technically could be endowed with similar capabilities, it is often uneconomic to do so. Therefore, any man–machine system will draw heavily on these comparative advantages of man.

The computer's range of superiority over man is well known to the point of triteness. All of its advantages rest on its ability to handle massive quantities of data with great speed, reliability, and accuracy. But these characteristics, when coupled with the flexibility and logical capabilities inherent in the stored-program computer, make it risky to invest man with permanent superiority over the computer in any sphere.

As is so often pointed out, in a literal sense the computer can do only what man directs it to do. Such a statement really implies only that the computer is a deterministic machine; it does not mean that the computer is forever limited to routine tasks that man himself has mastered. It is relatively easy, for example, to devise a computer program that can be comprehended at the detailed level, but which interacts in unpredictable ways with equally simple subprograms.

Since presumably man's brain is subject to the same sort of physical laws that govern the design of a computer, we have no evidence to support the view that man's mental endowments cannot be duplicated on the computer. Pattern recognition, associative memory, learning, intelligence, and even originality all have been demonstrated in at least primitive form. To be sure, in exhibiting these capabilities the computer merely slavishly follows orders in idiot-like fashion; but the results may appear indistinguishable from intelligence (if not wisdom), even to the creator of the computer's program.

The man–machine relationship must thus be a changing one. The allocation of tasks between the two components depends on the extent to which

[25] See, for example, Woodson and Conover (1964), p. 123.

man has been able to formulate problems in a way that can ultimately be
translated into detailed machine instructions. A key to success in this is a
language hierarchy that permits higher-level tasks to be defined in terms of
lower-level tasks.

The power of hierarchical languages is perhaps manifested most clearly
in mathematics. An axiomatic system provides a hierarchical structure with
which complex theorems can be generated from previously proved theorems.
Once proved, a new theorem becomes part of an extended language. It
can be used thereafter as a primitive element, without regard to its antecedent theorems. In the field of matrix algebra, for example, one can
manipulate matrices as algebraic entities rather than as complex arrays of
more primitive elements. The compression of past details into a compact
notation represents an extremely powerful way of extending man's ability
to think about complex problems.

This concept is employed routinely in computer programming. Computer languages are commonly defined in terms of a lower-level language.
Whole computer systems can be constructed in the form of a hierarchy of
subroutines (Emery, 1962). Any man–machine system must provide for
the continual extension of the computer's role through a hierarchical specification of its task. This allows, as it were, each version to be built on the
foundation of its predecessors. It is impossible for us to say now just how
high such an edifice can reach.

Man–Machine Planning Processes

The meager evidence that we have suggests that a symbiosis between
man and computer will prove especially powerful and fruitful in coping
with the enormously complex problems encountered in higher-level organizational planning (Morton, 1967). To the human component in a man–
machine planning system is relegated the responsibility for proposing
alternative plans and placing a utility value on the predicted consequences.
The machine is assigned the computational task of determining, by means
of a formal model, the consequences of each alternative.

A formalized planning model is used by the computer to transform decision variables into outcome variables. Normally this requires that the
computer make a number of routine "decisions." For example, in determining the consequences of a proposed increase in the aggregate production rate, the computer must make some assumptions about the allocation of
production capacity. In doing this, the computer should distribute production in an "optimal" fashion subject to the specified aggregate-capacity

constraint. On the basis of these detailed decisions, the computer can then determine such outcome variables as manufacturing costs and expected stockouts.

In addition to performing the transformation of decision variables into outcome variables, the computer should also provide a general capability for retrieving specified information. In formulating a plan, for example, the planners might want to know the value of such basic planning data as sales forecasts, available capacity, current inventories, and the like. In short, the planner should be able to quiz the computer about any detailed aspect of the formal planning model.

In such a system the computer serves as an extension to the mind of the planner. It offers the great advantage that complete formalization of the total decision process is not required. Those decisions and utility functions that are well understood and capable of being described formally can be incorporated into the computer model. Decisions and utilities that cannot be so formalized are simply reserved for the human decision maker.

As the planner gains greater understanding of the process, he can assign to the computer tasks that he formerly had to handle himself. The role of the human is not simply to make decisions about specific plans; he should also continually formalize the process of reaching these decisions. (The specification of decision processes represents, of course, a form of higher-level planning.)

Advantages of Man–Machine Planning[26]

Man–machine planning will have much the same character as any planning. For example, man–machine planning models, like the less formal ones, will have a hierarchical structure (Simon, 1960, pp. 49–50; Manheim, 1964). Factoring will be necessary, as before, in order to break up the global task into manageable subtasks. This fragmentation obviously introduces problems of coordination. Nevertheless, the problems are much less severe with man–machine systems than with conventional planning.

For one thing, the global task need not be fragmented to the same extent as before, since the computer can handle much greater complexity than the unaided planner. In effect, each model can have a wide "span of control," thereby reducing the number of submodels and the hierarchical depth of global planning. Suboptimization will still occur, but the more comprehensive nature of the planning models will reduce the penalties typically associated with this process.

[26] Carroll (1966) and Zannetos (1968) provide additional comments on this subject.

Any man–machine model should have a hierarchical structure that allows the planner to examine details selectively. He can first formulate a high-level plan by means of a sequential search through a low-resolution plan space described by an aggregate model. Upon finding a satisfactory plan, he can then explore the plan in greater depth by using more detailed, higher-resolution models.

In addition, the enormous input–output capacity of modern computers permits a relatively close link of a computer model with the global data base of the organization. Every planner therefore can have much closer access to the plans of other organizational units included in the data base. This will greatly facilitate the coordination of activities throughout the organization, thereby further reducing the penalties of suboptimization (Carroll, 1967b).

Computer models will not change the iterative nature of planning. This scheme provides an efficient means of communicating between hierarchical levels in formalized as well as conventional planning. However, man–machine iterative planning can offer the advantage of explicitly identifying unrealistic high-level plans during the detailed amplification by lower-level models. As a result, the high-level planner can make appropriate modifications to his plan before an attempt is made to execute it. In conventional systems, such modification may not be made until long afterwards, when an exception message identifies deviations in an unrealistic plan.

A man–machine system offers the obvious advantage of speeding up all phases of the planning process. Plans can thus be formulated on the basis of more recent information about the state of nature. Greater speed in planning also permits quicker response to changes in existing plans if that should prove necessary. Normally of far greater importance, the computer's speed permits relatively quick response to the planner's *proposed* plans. This allows him to evaluate a larger number of alternative plans and to retain a closer grasp of a complex problem over the reduced response interval.

The relatively low cost of processing information in a man–machine system will induce a change in the balance between the cost and value of additional planning. The economic balance point will shift sharply toward the use of greater detail in planning, the consideration of more alternatives, the introduction of greater realism in models, and more frequent replanning.

Finally, man–machine planning will permit a high-level planner to maintain far greater touch with detailed planning than he can with conventional systems. If he participates in the development of the models by which his aggregate decisions are amplified into detailed plans, a planner can formulate high-level plans with a reasonable confidence that the resulting low-level plans will be satisfactory.[27] Furthermore, access to a common data base allows a planner to monitor the execution of his plan by lower-level units.

In the absence of a sophisticated planning system, the planner has little assurance that his plans will be executed faithfully. A great deal of "noise" is introduced during execution. Lower levels in the organization have a vast catalogue of ways to frustrate the execution of grand strategy, most of which are evoked out of misunderstanding, confusion, and as protection against poor higher-level planning. Computer-based planning will certainly not eliminate these problems, but it can mitigate them.

An argument can be raised that a manager should be denied access to detailed information about performance more than one or two levels below him in the organizational hierarchy. The claim might be that such access subverts the regular lines of responsibility and swamps the higher-level manager in needless detail. This is a difficult position to defend.

First, obtaining information about lower-level performance does not at all preclude management through regular channels. To be sure, the relationship between a manager and a subordinate might well be altered in an environment in which the manager can monitor directly the execution of plans. However, it is untenable to take the position that this relationship can thrive only on ignorance stemming from the subordinate's filtering out information that should reach his superior.

Second, a high-level manager cannot indiscriminately poke around in the detailed operation of his organization, regardless of the information-processing facilities at his disposal. There is simply too much information for him to comprehend more than a small fraction of it. Therefore he must be exceedingly selective in the information he scans.

He must rely heavily on the information system to screen out all irrelevant data. If, however, the system reveals a problem that has occurred at a lower level, the high-level manager should have ready access to information required to analyze the problem in sufficient detail to determine *the action appropriate at his level*. If a "detail" assumes enough importance to be brought to the attention of the manager, then it ceases to be a detail. The lower-level supervisor responsible for the problem can hardly plead immunity to such examination on the grounds that it represents unjustified meddling.

---

[27] The planner obviously cannot know all of the technical details of a model, but he should be very much aware of the major concepts underlying it. This requirement places a premium on a planner's active participation, at the policy level, in the development of the models he uses.

It is only fair to point out, however, that any powerful technology is always subject to abuse. The opposition that exists to the development of complex information systems stems in large measure from a conviction that we cannot intelligently implement and administer them. There is plenty of evidence to support this view.

This need not be the case if we recognize the limitations of such systems. Any information system provides a very abstract and imperfect view of reality, and so its output must be interpreted with understanding and humility. Before any harsh action is taken to correct a deviation in a plan, the person held responsible should be allowed some form of due process. This will reduce the risk of attaching too much weight to incomplete, inaccurate, or misleading formal measures of performance. Furthermore, the system should undergo continual improvement and adaptation as errors and shortcomings are brought to light. Anything short of these safeguards can easily lead to dull conformity and gross injustice.

Modification of the Man–Machine System to Achieve Organizational Adaptation

Man–machine planning has as its purpose the location of a satisfactory plan. The choice is limited to the set of all alternatives that can be generated and described by the algorithms and variables used in the planning model available to the planner. This set by no means includes all "real" alternatives, since not every possible alternative can be generated by a given planning model. The plan space defined by abstract decision and outcome variables represents only an infinitesimal portion of the organization's "real" plan space. Furthermore, only a very small fraction of the points included in even this reduced space remains accessible to the planner. For example, the model will not generate an inventory distribution that is nonoptimal in terms of the model's algorithm for allocating aggregate production.

The planner naturally seeks improved plans out of the real alternatives available to him, and not just the potential candidates found in the space of the existing planning model. This does not mean, however, that he should have complete access to every conceivable alternative. On the contrary, the very purpose of the planning model is to confine the planner's search to a "good" region of the real space, and to exclude "bad"—and, therefore, irrelevant—portions. The planner must aim at improving the model so that it provides access to *fewer* but *better* alternatives.[28]

[28] The ideal model makes accessible only a single plan—the optimum one in terms of real alternatives, real goals, and the real state of nature.

This philosophy should lead the planner to employ modifications in the planning model as the predominant mechanism for generating improved plans. The planning model should be highly *parameterized* to facilitate these changes. For example, an inventory-control algorithm should include a carrying-cost parameter that can be modified readily (assuming that the specification of carrying cost cannot be formalized and included in the model). If a temporary shortage of funds within the organization forces a reduction in inventory, the planner can accomplish this by increasing the carrying-cost parameter. The "knob" to adjust the parameter can simply be turned until a satisfactory level of inventory is found through a trial-and-error process. The system can aid the planner in setting the parameter value by providing him with information such as the implied tradeoff between inventory dollars and the expected number of stockouts.

A change in an algorithm represents a more basic type of modification in the planning model than does a change in its parameters. For example, an algorithm for determining inventory decisions might be revised to include some refinement—the explicit consideration of capacity constraints, say. The planning model should be designed to permit great flexibility in making such changes. This can be done, for instance, by the use of modular programs and higher-level languages.

Even more fundamental changes in the planning model can be made. For example, the structure of the model may be altered by combining two or more activities that previously were planned independently. This might occur, say, when the scheduling of two factories is combined in order to find joint optimum schedules instead of independently suboptimized schedules. Changes of this sort provide the basis for long-range adaptation and fundamental improvement (Pounds, 1963). They depend on the judgment and creativity that only man is (currently) capable of supplying (Ackoff, 1967).

5.9 *Conclusions*

The conclusions of this book can be stated rather simply. The time now seems ripe for a major improvement in organizational planning. Information technology has advanced to a point that large man–machine planning systems are technically and economically feasible. Such a system could provide major improvements in the planning process.

The effect on organizational behavior could be profound. The planning process largely governs behavior, and therefore fundamental improvements in performance must come principally through better planning. By permitting closer coordination among organizational subunits, improved planning leads to a more consistent pursuit of global goals and results in fewer resources devoted to cushioning the effects of fragmented activities.

Organizational planning is so enormously complex that a major improvement in the process will require massive data handling. The planner must have a means of collecting, transmitting, storing, retrieving, manipulating, and displaying very large quantities of information. And he must be able to do all of this with great generality and flexibility.

A planning system must be capable of exploiting the capabilities of the human planner as well as the data-handling capacity of the computer. Man's ability to reason, improvise, make judgments, and recognize complex patterns makes him an essential contributor to high-level planning. The interface between the man and the machine must therefore facilitate communications in order to foster a close rapport between the two. In this way the system can tap the best features of both man and machine.

A man–machine planning system centered around a common data base seems technically capable of providing the required logical and data-handling capabilities. Advances in information technology—manifested in both computer hardware and software—now permit reasonably effective management of the required masses of data. There thus appears to be no major block to the development of comprehensive man–machine planning systems.

Such a system will obviously not be easy to implement. Without question it will involve a great deal of time, effort, and expense. But what are the alternatives? The organization currently pays an inordinate price for planning. It pays in the form of the costs required to sustain its present planning "model"—the organizational hierarchy engaged in the amplification of high-level plans into more detailed form. It also pays in the form of unnecessarily poor performance.

The generation of substantially better plans is so complex a task that only through an elaborate man–machine system can we hope to come to grips with it. Such a system will provide an efficient means of performing a sequential, iterative search through a hierarchical plan space of the organization.

Bibliography

ACKOFF, R. L. 1961. Systems, organizations, and interdisciplinary research. In Donald P. Eckman (ed.), *Systems: research and design*. Proceedings of the first systems symposium at Case Institute of Technology, pp. 26–42. John Wiley & Sons, New York.

ACKOFF, R. L., 1962. *Scientific method: optimizing applied research decisions*. John Wiley & Sons, New York.

ACKOFF, R. L. 1963. General systems theory and systems research contrasting conceptions of systems science. *General Systems*, **VIII**, 117–121.

ACKOFF, R. L. 1967. Management misinformation systems. *Management Science*, **14, 4** (December 1967), B147–B156.

ALEXANDER, CHRISTOPHER. 1964. *Notes on the synthesis of form*. Harvard University Press, Cambridge, Mass.

ALEXANDER, SIDNEY S. 1962. Income measurement in a dynamic economy. In W. T. Baxter and Sidney Davidson, *Studies in accounting theory* (2nd ed.) Richard D. Irwin, Homewood, Ill.

ANDO, ALBERT, and FRANKLIN M. FISHER. 1963. Near-decomposability, partition and aggregation, and the relevance of stability discussions. *International Economic Review*, **4, 1** (January 1963), 53–67.

ANTHONY, ROBERT N. 1965. *Planning and control systems: a framework for analysis*. Division of Research, Graduate School of Business, Harvard University, Boston.

ARROW, KENNETH J. 1959. Optimization, decentralization, and internal pricing in business firms. In *Contributions to scientific research in management*. Graduate School of Business Administration, U.C.L.A., Los Angeles.

ASHBY, W. ROSS. 1956. *An introduction to cybernetics*. Chapman & Hall, London.

ASHBY, W. ROSS. 1963. Cybernetics today and its future contributions to the engineering-sciences. *General Systems*, **VIII**, 207–212.

ASHBY, W. ROSS. 1964. The next ten years. In J. T. Tou and R. H. Wilcox, *Computer and information sciences*, pp. 2–11. Spartan Books, Washington, D.C.

BELLMAN, RICHARD. 1961. A mathematical formulation of variational process of adaptive type. *Proceedings of the fourth Berkeley symposium*, **I**, 37–48. University of California Press, Berkeley.

BISHOP, G. H. 1960. Feedback through the environment as an analog of brain functioning. In M. C. Yovits and S. Cameron (eds.), *Self-organizing systems*, pp. 122–146. Pergamon Press, New York.

BLANNING, ROBERT W. 1967. The value and cost of information. Paper presented at the A.I.I.E. Conference on Management Information Systems, October 26, 1967, Rochester, N.Y.

BOULDING, KENNETH E. 1956. *The image*. University of Michigan Press, Ann Arbor.

BOWMAN, E. H. 1963. Consistency and optimality in managerial decision making. *Management Science*, **9, 2** (June 1963), 310–321.

BOYD, D. F., and H. S. KRASNOW. 1963. Economic evaluation of management information systems. *IBM Systems Journal*, **2** (March 1963), 2–23.

BRANCH, MELVILLE C. 1966. *Planning: aspects and applications*. John Wiley & Sons, New York.

BREMERMANN, H. J. 1962. Optimization through evaluation and recombination. In

M. C. Yovits, G. T. Jocobi, and G. D. Goldstirn (eds.), *Self-organizing systems*, pp. 93–106. Spartan Press, Washington, D.C.

BURKHEAD, JESSE. 1956. *Government budgeting.* Wiley, New York.

CARROLL, DONALD C. 1965. *Heuristic sequencing of single and multiple component jobs.* Unpublished Ph.D. thesis, M.I.T., Cambridge, Mass.

CARROLL, DONALD C. 1966. Man–machine cooperation on planning and control problems. *Industrial Management Review,* **8, 1** (Fall 1966), 47–54.

CARROLL, DONALD C. 1967a. On the structure of operational control systems. In John F. Pierce, Jr. (ed.), *Operations research and design of management information systems,* pp. 391–415. Badger Printing Corporation, Appleton, Wisc.

CARROLL, DONALD C. 1967b. Implications of on-line, real-time systems for managerial decision making. In *The Management of Aerospace Programs,* pp. 345–370. American Astronautical Society, Tarzana, Calif.

CARROLL, DONALD C., and Z. S. ZANNETOS. 1967. Toward the realization of intelligent management information systems. In Walker, pp. 151–167.

CHESTNUT, HAROLD. 1967. *Systems engineering tools.* John Wiley & Sons, New York.

CRAIK, K. J. W. 1943. *The nature of explanation.* Cambridge University Press, Cambridge, England.

CYERT, R. D., and J. G. MARCH. 1963. *A behavioral theory of the firm.* Prentice-Hall, Englewood Cliffs, N.J.

DANZIS, ALAN L. 1965. *A real-time computer system for order-entry and inventory control.* Unpublished masters thesis, M.I.T., Cambridge, Mass.

DEARDON, JOHN. 1964. Can management information be automated? *Harvard Business Review,* **42, 2** (March/April 1964), 128–135.

EDP Analyzer, Canning Publications, Vista, California.

May 1965.	New approaches to random access files.
June 1965.	A new look in management reporting.
August 1965.	Significant progress in optical scanning.
October 1965.	Generalized file processing software.
February 1966.	New views on mass storage.
August 1966.	Trends in corporate data systems.
November 1966.	The corporate data file.
December 1966.	Corporate data file design.
January 1967.	New management reporting systems.
February 1967.	Advances in fast response systems.
April 1967.	Building corporate data systems.
December 1967.	Data management: file organization.
January 1968.	Data management: functions.

EMERY, J. C. 1960. Control of finished goods inventory. In C. West Churchman and Michael Verhulst (eds.), *Management science—models and techniques* **I,** 560–576. Pergamon Press, New York.

EMERY, J. C. 1961. An approach to job shop scheduling using a large-scale computer. *Industrial Management Review,* **3, 1** (Fall 1961), 78–96.

EMERY, J. C. 1962. Modular data processing systems written in COBOL. *Communications of the ACM,* **5, 5** (May 1962), 263–268.

EMERY, J. C. 1964. The impact of information technology on organization. In *Proceedings of the 24th annual meeting,* Academy of Management, Chicago, 1964, pp. 69–78. Reprinted in Peter P. Schoderbek, *Management Systems,* pp. 94–101. John Wiley & Sons, New York.

EMERY, J. C. 1965. *Organizational planning and control: theory and technology,* Ph.D. Thesis, M.I.T., Cambridge, Mass.

EMERY, J. C., and D. N. NESS. 1968. A man–machine budgeting system. In C. H. Kriebel and R. L. Van Horn (eds.), *Management information systems: progress and perspectives,* proceedings of a research symposium held at Carnegie-Mellon University, Pittsburgh, June 1968.

159

FORRESTER, JAY W. 1961. *Industrial dynamics*. John Wiley & Sons, New York.

GARDNER, JOHN W. 1964. *Self-renewal*. Harper & Row, New York.

GOETZ, B. E. 1949. *Management planning and control*. McGraw-Hill, New York.

GOETZ, B. E. 1965. *Quantitative methods*. McGraw-Hill, New York.

GOODE, H. H., and R. E. MACHOL. 1957. *Systems engineering—an introduction to the design of large-scale systems*. McGraw-Hill, New York.

GORDON, MYRON J. 1964. The use of administered price systems to control large organizations. In C. P. Bonini, R. K. Jaedicke, and H. M. Wagner (eds.), *Management controls: new directions in basic research*, pp. 1–26. McGraw-Hill, New York.

GRAICUNAS, V. A. 1937. Relationship in organization. In Luther Gulick and L. Urwick (eds.), *Papers in the science of administration*. Institute of Public Administration, New York, pp. 183–187. Originally published in the *Bulletin of the International Management Institute*, International Labor Office, Geneva, March 1933.

GRANT, E. E., and H. SACKMAN. 1967. An exploratory investigation of programmer performance under on-line and off-line conditions. *IEEE Transactions on Human Factors in Electronics*, **HFE–8, 1** (March 1967), 33–48.

GREEN, B. F., et al. 1961. Baseball: an automatic question-answerer. *Proceedings of the Western Joint Computer Conference*, **19** (May 1961), pp. 219–224.

GREGORY, R. H. and VAN HORN, R. L. 1963. *Automatic data-processing systems* (2nd ed.) Wadsworth Publishing Co., Belmont, Calif.

HABERSTROH, CHADWICK. 1958. *Process of internal control in firms*. Unpublished Ph.D. thesis, University of Minnesota, Minneapolis.

HALL, ARTHUR D. 1962. *Systems engineering*. D. Van Nostrand, Princeton, N.J.

HAMMER, CARL. 1967. Software considerations for information systems and operations analysis. In Walker, pp. 11–17.

HITCH, CHARLES J. 1953. Suboptimization in operations problems. *Journal of the Operations Research Society of America*, **1, 3** (May 1953), 87–99.

HITCH, C. J., and R. N. MCKEAN. 1960. *The economics of defense in the nuclear age*. Harvard University Press, Cambridge, Mass.

HOLT, C., et al., 1960. *Planning production, inventories, and work force*. Prentice-Hall, Englewood Cliffs, N.J.

HUGHES, CHARLES L. 1965. *Goal setting*. American Management Association, New York.

JOHNSON, R. A., F. E. KAST, and J. E. ROSENZWEIG. 1967. *The theory and management of systems* (2nd ed.) McGraw-Hill, New York.

KLAHR, CARL N. 1958. Multiple objectives in mathematical programming. *Operations Research*, **6, 6** (November/December 1958), 849–855.

KNIGHT, KENNETH E. 1966. Changes in computer performance. *Datamation*, **12, 9**, (September 1966), 40–54.

KNIGHT, KENNETH E. 1968. Evolving computer performance—1963–1967. *Datamation*, **14, 1** (January 1968), 31–35.

KOONTZ, H. D., and C. J. O'DONNELL. 1964. *Principles of management* (3rd ed.) McGraw-Hill, New York.

LEDLEY, ROBERT S. 1962. *Programming and utilizing digital computers*. McGraw-Hill, New York.

LICKLIDER, J. C. R. 1960. Man–computer symbiosis. *IRE Transactions on Human Factors in Electronics*, **HFE-1** (March 1960), 4–10.

LIKERT, RENSIS. 1961. *New patterns of management*. McGraw-Hill, New York.

MCDONOUGH, ADRIAN M. 1963. *Information economics and management systems*. McGraw-Hill, New York.

MANHEIM, M. L. 1964. *Highway route location as a hierarchically structured sequential decision process*. Ph.D. thesis, M.I.T., Cambridge, Mass.

MARCH, J. G., and H. A. SIMON. 1958. *Organizations*. John Wiley & Sons, New York.

MARSCHAK, JACOB. 1954. Toward an economic theory of organization and information. Cowles Commission Paper, New Series, No. 95, University of Chicago.

MARSCHAK, JACOB. 1959a. Remarks on the economics of information. In *Contributions to scientific research in management.* Graduate School of Business Administration, U.C.L.A., Los Angeles, pp. 79–98.

MARSCHAK, JACOB. 1959b. Efficient and viable organizational forms. In Maison Haire (ed.), *Modern organization theory.* John Wiley & Sons, New York.

MARSCHAK, JACOB. 1962. Problems in information economics: general concepts, and a case of increasing returns to information. Working Paper No. 24, Western Management Science Institute, U.C.L.A., Los Angeles.

MARSCHAK, JACOB. 1963. The payoff-relevant description of states and acts. *Econometrica,* **31, 4** (October 1963), 719–725.

MARTIN, JAMES. 1967. *Design of real-time computer systems.* Prentice-Hall, Englewood Cliffs, N.J.

MATHEWS, M. V. 1968. Choosing a scientific computer for service. *Science,* **161, 3836** (July 5, 1968), 23–27.

MESAROVIC, MIHAJLO D. 1962. On self organizational systems. In M. C. Yovits, G. T. Jocobi, and G. D. Goldstein (eds.), *Self-organizing systems,* pp. 9–36. Spartan Press, Washington, D.C.

MILLER, D. W., and M. K. STARR. 1960. *Executive decisions and operations research.* Prentice-Hall, Englewood Cliffs, N.J.

MILLER, GEORGE A. 1956. The magical number seven, plus or minus two: some limits on our capacity for processing information. *Psychological Review,* **63, 2** (March 1956), 81–97.

MINKER, JACK, and JEROME SABLE. 1967. *Annual Review of Information and Technology.* American Documentation Institute, Interscience Publishers, New York, Chapter 7.

MINSKY, MARVIN. 1961. Steps toward artificial intelligence. *Proceedings of the I.R.E.,* **49, 1** (January 1961), 8–30. Reprinted in E. A. Feigenbaum and J. Feldman (eds.), *Computers and thought.* McGraw-Hill, New York, 1963.

MORRIS, WILLIAM T. 1968. *Decentralization in management systems.* Ohio State University Press, Columbus.

MORTON, MICHAEL S. S. 1967. Interactive visual display systems and management problem solving. *Industrial Management Review,* **9, 1** (Fall 1967), 69–81.

MUTH, JOHN F. 1963. The effect of uncertainty in job times on optimal schedules. In J. F. Muth and G. L. Thompson (eds.), *Industrial Scheduling,* pp. 300–307. Prentice-Hall, Englewood Cliffs, N.J.

NAUR, PETER (ed.) 1963. Revised report on the algorithmic language ALGOL 60. *Communications of the ACM,* **6, 1** (January 1963), 1–17.

NEWELL, A., J. C. SHAW, and H. A. SIMON. 1959. *The process of creative thinking.* RAND document P–1320 (September 1958, revised January 1959). The RAND Corporation, Santa Monica, Calif.

NEWMAN, W. H. 1951. *Administrative action—the techniques of organization and management.* Prentice-Hall, New York.

POSTLEY, JOHN A. 1968. The Mark IV System. *Datamation,* **14, 1** (January 1968), 28–30.

POUNDS, WILLIAM F. 1963. The scheduling environment. In J. F. Muth and G. L. Thompson (eds.), *Industrial scheduling,* pp. 5–12. Prentice-Hall, Englewood Cliffs.

POWERS, W. T., R. K. CLARK, and R. I. McFARLAND. 1960. A general feedback theory of human behavior. *General Systems,* **V,** 63–83.

Programming system for the office of the secretary of defense. 1962. Department of Defense, U.S. Government Printing Office, Washington, D.C. (June 1962).

PURCELL, EDWARD. 1963. Parts and wholes in physics. In Daniel Lerner (ed.), *Parts and wholes,* pp. 11–39. The Free Press, New York.

ROME, SIDNEY, and BEATRICE ROME. 1962a. Computer simulations toward a theory of large organizations. In Borko, Harold (ed.), *Computer applications in the behavioral sciences,* pp. 522–555. Prentice-Hall, Englewood Cliffs, N.J.

ROME, SIDNEY, and BEATRICE ROME. 1962b. Leviathan: an experimental study of large organizations with the aid of computers. *Proceedings of the First Congress on Information System Sciences,* November 1962, Session 7, pp. 1–87.

SAMUEL, A. L. 1959. Some studies in machine learning using the game of checkers. *IBM Journal of Research and Development*, **2, 7** (July 1959), 211–229. Reprinted in E. A. Feigenbaum and J. Feldman (eds.), *Computers and thought*, 1963, pp. 71–105. McGraw-Hill, New York.

SCHLAIFER, ROBERT. 1961. *Introduction to statistics for business decisions.* McGraw-Hill, New York.

SCHLEH, EDWARD C. 1961. *Management by results.* McGraw-Hill, New York.

SHERIDAN, T. B., et al. 1964. Control models of creatures which look ahead. *Proceeding of the fifth national symposium on human factors in electronics*, May 5–6, 1964, pp. 229–240. Institute of Electrical and Electronic Engineers, New York.

SIMON, HERBERT A. 1960. *The new science of management.* Harper & Row, New York.

SIMON, HERBERT A. 1962. The architecture of complexity. *Proceedings American Philosophical Society*, **106, 6** (December 1962), 467–482.

SIMON, HERBERT A. 1964. On the concept of organizational goal. *Administrative Science Quarterly*, **9, 1** (June 1964), 1–22.

SIMON, H. A. and A. ANDO. 1961. Aggregation of variables in dynamic systems. *Econometrica*, **29, 2** (April 1961), 111–138.

SISSON, ROGER L. 1960. An appraisal of current computer applications. In D. G. Malcolm and A. J. Rowe (eds.), *Management control systems*. John Wiley & Sons, New York.

STARR, MARTIN KENNETH. 1964. *Production management—systems and synthesis.* Prentice-Hall, Englewood Cliffs, N.J.

STEDRY, A. C. 1962. *Budget control and cost behavior.* Prentice-Hall, Englewood Cliffs, N.J.

SUMMERS, J. K., and EDWARD BENNETT. 1967. AESOP—A final report: a prototype on-line interactive information control system. In Walker, pp. 69–86.

TAUBERT, WILLIAM H. 1968. A search decision rule for the aggregate scheduling problem. *Management Science*, **14, 6** (February 1968), B343–B359.

TAYLOR, ROBERT W. 1967. Man–computer input-output techniques. *IEEE Transactions on Human Factors in Electronics*, **HFE–8, 1** (March 1967), 1–4.

THEIL, H. 1961. *Economic forecasts and policy* (2nd ed.) North-Holland Publishing Co., Amsterdam.

THEIL, H. 1964. *Optimal decision rules for government and industry.* North-Holland Publishing Co., Amsterdam.

WALKER, DONALD E. (ed.) 1967. *Information system science and technology.* Thompson Book Co., Washington, D.C.

WHINSTON, ANDREW. 1962. *Price coordination in decentralized systems.* Unpublished Ph.D. thesis, Graduate School of Industrial Administration, Carnegie Institute of Technology, Pittsburgh.

WILDE, DOUGLASS J. 1964. *Optimum seeking methods.* Prentice-Hall, Englewood Cliffs, N.J.

WILLIAMS, T. J. 1968. Computer systems for industrial process control—a review of progress, needs, and expected developments. *Proceedings of IFIP Congress 68*, pp. E1–E11. Edinburgh, Scotland.

WILLIAMSON, OLIVER E. 1967. Hierarchical control and optimum firm size. *Journal of Political Economy*, **75, 2** (April 1967), 123–138.

WOODSON, W. E., and D. W. CONOVER. 1964. *Human engineering guide for equipment designers.* University of California Press, Berkeley.

YING, CHARLES C. 1964. A dynamic model of information and organization. Unpublished paper.

ZANNETOS, ZENON S. 1965. On the theory of divisional structures: some aspects of centralization and decentralization of control and decision making. *Management Science*, **12, 4** (December 1965), B49–B68.

ZANNETOS, ZENON S. 1968. Toward intelligent management information systems. *Industrial Management Review*, **9, 3** (Spring 1968), 21–38.

Index

Ackoff, R. L., 1, 3, 42, 99, 136, 156
Adaptation, 125–26, 155–56
Aggregation of data, 42, 48–49, 137–38
Alexander, C., 2, 16, 17
Alexander, S. S., 115
Ando, A., 29, 31, 32
Anthony, R. N., 131
Arrow, K. J., 116n, 122
Ashby, W. R., 4, 8, 22, 25, 116

Bayesian analysis, 72–73
Bellman, R., 44
Bishop, G., 2, 114
Black box, as a component of system, 6
Blanning, R. W., 74, 91n
Boulding, K. E., 134
Bowman, E. H., 139n
Boyd, D. F., 66
Branch, M. C., 126
Bremermann, H. J., 8
Buffer, as a decoupling device, 26–27
Burkhead, J., 129

Carroll, D. C., 101, 145, 147, 148, 152n, 153
Centralization, 120–24
Certainty equivalent, 44
Clark, R. K., 1, 118n
Classification of data, 39–41
Collection of data, 36–39, 64
Communication, 11–12, 59–62
Computation, 58–59
Computer
  capabilities in a man-machine system, 149–51
  hardware and software for, 50n
Conover, D. W., 150n
Constraints in planning, 120–25
Control of a plan, 140–42
Coordination, 11–12, 28–31, 61, 65, 113–14
Cost
  of information, 66–67, 102–107, 149

of planning, 143, 148–49
Coupling among subsystems, 22
Craik, K. J., 134
Cyert, R. D., 127, 148

Danzis, A., 40n
Data
  aggregation, 42, 48–49, 137–38
  classification, 39–41
  collection, 36–39, 64
  compression, 41–44
  display, 62–63
  planning, 131–33
  probabilistic, 43–44
  retrieval, 50–56, 154
  storage, 44–49
  transmission, 59–62
Data base, 12n, 65
  inquiry to, 48–56, 99, 104, 113
  organization, 44–45
  security of, 56–57
Data management, 49–58
  systems for, 57–58
Deardon, J., 149
Decentralization, 120–24
Decision criteria, 73n
Decision variable, 110–12
Decomposable system, 29–33
Decoupling of subsystems, 24–28
Display of data, 62–63

Economy of scale in data processing, 60
Efficiency frontier, 135
Elementary system task, 6
Emery, J. C., 2, 8, 9, 12, 111, 121, 142, 147, 151
Exception reporting, 41–42, 99, 104

Feedback data, 140
Filtering by the information system, 41–42, 99, 101, 114, 154
Fisher, F. M., 29

Flexibility
  as a decoupling device, 27–28
  provided by an information system, 57, 102, 106–107
Forecasting, 100–101, 132–33
Forrester, J. W., 9, 62n, 102
Fragmentation of a system, 9–10

Gardner, J. W., 114
Generality provided by an information system, 102, 106
Goals, 115–18
  multidimensional, 115–17, 134–39
  surrogates for, 117–18
Goetz, B. E., 17n, 39, 40, 91n, 108, 111, 112n, 131, 139
Goode, H. H., 30
Gordon, M. J., 15n
Graicunas, V. A., 10
Grant, E. E., 101
Green, B. F., 51n
Gregory, R. H., 45n
Grosch's Law, 60

Haberstroh, C., 117, 137
Hall, A. D., 1, 2, 147
Hammer, C., 50n
Hierarchy of subsystems, 2n, 3
Hitch, C. J., 5, 134, 137, 138, 148
Holt, C., 133
Hughes, C. L., 117n

Indexing, 39–41, 51–52
Information
  cost of, 66–67, 102–107
  value of, 66–67, 73–76, 98–102, 142–48
    complete, 79–80
    difficulties in determining, 89–91
    partial, 80–86
    probabilistic, 86–89
Information system, 34–36
  accuracy, 101–102, 105–106
  detail provided by, 98–99, 103–104
  filtering by, 41–42, 99, 101, 114, 154
  flexibility, 57, 102, 106–107
  functions of, 36–63
  generality provided by, 102, 106
  integrated, 63–65
  reliability, 101, 102, 105–106
  response time, 100–101, 104–105, 148, 153
  selectivity, 41–42, 98–99, 101, 104, 114, 154
  structure of, 69–72
Inquiry to a data base, 48–56, 99, 104, 113
Integrated information systems, 63–65
Interactions among subsystems, 3–4, 21–28
  reducing, 23–28
  sources of, 21–23
Interface between subsystems, 3

Johnson, R. A., 1

Kast, F. E., 1
Klahr, C. N., 136
Knight, K. E., 60n
Koontz, H. D., 109
Krasnow, H. S., 66

Ledley, R. S., 53
Licklider, J. C. R., 63
Likert, R., 116

Machol, R. E., 30
Manheim, M. L., 2, 129, 152
Man-machine planning systems, 149–56
  man's capabilities in, 149–51
March, J. G., 6, 24, 35, 43, 109, 110n, 120, 127, 138, 148
Marschak, J., 67, 71
Martin, J., 63n, 100n, 106
Mathews, M. V., 61
McDonough, A. M., 3n
McFarland, R. I., 1, 118n
McKean, R. N., 5, 134, 137, 138, 148
Mesarovic, M. D., 118, 126
Miller, D. W., 40, 73n
Miller, G. A., 11, 137
Minker, J., 58n
Minsky, M., 125n
Model, use in planning, 134, 151–52, 156
Morris, W. T., 19, 109, 125
Morton, M. S. S., 151
Muth, J. F., 44

Naur, P., 52n
Ness, D. N., 142
Newell, A., 2, 17
Newman, W. H., 108, 109

O'Donnell, C. J., 109
Organization
 hierarchical structure of, 20–21
 viewed as a system, 20–32
Outcome variable, 110–12

Payoff matrix, 67–69
Plan
 alternative, 133–34
 control of, 140–42
 description of actions and outcomes,
 108–13
 imperfections in, 142–43
 motivating effects, 115–18
 selection of optimum, 134–39
 vehicle of coordination, 28–29, 65,
 113–14
Planning
 bottom-up, 126–29
 cost of, 143, 148–49
 data for, 131–33
 geometric interpretation, 129–31
 hierarchical nature, 118–26, 152–53
 iterative nature, 126–29, 153
 man-machine, 149–56
 steps in, 131–42
 top-down, 118–26
 use of model in, 134, 151–52, 156
 value, 143–148
Postley, J. A., 52n
Pounds, W. F., 156
Powers, W. T., 1, 118n
Prediction, 100–101, 132–33, 148
Probabilistic data, 43–44
Purcell, E., 4

Random processing, 59
Reliability provided by an information
 system, 101, 102, 105–106
Response time provided by an information
 system, 100–101, 104–105, 148, 153
Retrieval of data, 50–56, 154
Rome, B., 36n, 55
Rome, S., 36n, 55
Rosenzweig, J. E., 1

Sable, J., 58n
Sackman, H., 101
Samuel, A. L., 116n
Satisficing search strategy, 138

Schlaifer, R., 72n
Schleh, E. C., 118, 137
Security of the data base, 56–57
Selectivity provided by an information
 system, 41–42, 98–99, 101, 104, 114,
 154
Sensitivity analysis, 91–98
Sequential processing, 59
Shaw, J. C., 2, 17
Sheridan, T. B., 145
Simon, H. A., 2, 4, 6, 11, 17, 24, 29, 31,
 32, 35, 36, 43, 109, 110n, 114n, 120,
 121, 126, 138, 152
Sisson, R. L., 62, 129
Span of control, 9–11
 effect on fragmentation, 10
Standardization, as a decoupling device,
 26
Starr, M. K., 40, 73n, 81, 127
Stedry, A. C., 128n
Storage of data, 44–49
Structure of a system, 5–19
Suboptimization, 5, 10, 24–25, 122, 152
Subsystems
 hierarchy of, 2n, 3
 interactions among, 3–4, 21–28
 interface between, 3
System
 boundary of, 4–5
 characteristics, 1–5
 for data management, 57–58
 decomposable, 29–33
 environment, 4–5
 factoring into subsystems, 6
 fragmentation of, 9–10
 structure, 5–19
  criteria for choosing, 13–16
  heuristics for designing, 17–19
  number of alternatives, 7–8
  optimum, 16–17

Taubert, W. H., 134
Taylor, R. W., 63
Theil, H., 44
Tradeoff
 among multidimensional goals, 115,
 134–39
 subsystem independence versus coordi-
 nation, 29–31
Transfer prices, 15n, 123n
Transmission of data, 59–62

Uncertainty absorption, 43
Utility function, 115, 136, 139

Van Horn, R. L., 45n

Whinston, A., 116
Wilde, D. J., 134

Williams, T. J., 118n, 124
Williamson, O. E., 118
Woodson, W. E., 150n

Ying, C. C., 67

Zannetos, Z. S., 126, 152n